The Happy Place

By Lori Gosselin

Revised edition © 2016 by Lori Gosselin

Original edition © 2011 by Lori Gosselin

ISBN-10:
0987684027

ISBN-13:
978-0987684028

To my mother
who celebrated and treasured me
always
and to my daughter
who helped me
to remember

CONTENTS

1

The Beginning

"'Who in the world am I?
Ah, that's the great puzzle!"
~ Alice in Wonderland ~
Lewis Carroll

Do you ever wake in the morning feeling sad or "off," and
you don't know why? Do you wonder how you can already
be feeling *anything* when you haven't even had time to
think? I used to feel this way every morning. I thought it was
normal. My usual response was this: think about the day
ahead, search for something good to look forward to, and
stack these better feelings on top of the bad feelings until I
didn't feel the negative ones anymore.

It never occurred to me to wonder why I awoke this way. For
me, mornings had been like this for as long as I could
remember. I accepted these morning feelings as little battles
I had to fight. I was good at fighting them. After I had dealt
with them, I never gave them any thought at all.

While the morning feelings did not make it onto my list of feelings to examine, many others did. I was adept at facing my feelings and doing something about them. I sought to understand them.

Anthony de Mello, Jesuit Priest, psychotherapist and writer, often said *awareness is everything.* I had noticed that as soon as I understood why I felt a certain way, I would feel quite a bit better. "Knowing is 90% of the healing!" I used to say. But what about the other 10%?

What do we do when we know *why* we feel the way we do, but the "knowing" doesn't make the bad feeling go away? What do we do about the morning feelings and other unwanted feelings that are too low on the radar to merit professional attention, but too prevalent and painful to ignore?

The answers to all these questions came to me while I was traveling in Europe with my daughter. But the story began long before the wheels of the plane touched the runway on the other side of the ocean.

2

The Story

"Make your choice, adventurous stranger;
Strike the bell and bide the danger,
Or wonder, till it drives you mad,
What would have followed if you had."
~ The Magician's Nephew ~
C.S. Lewis

My Parents said I was a contented child. Perhaps I was. I was happy for most of my life, or so I thought. When my fiancé lost his job four months before our already-planned wedding, we decided that he would join me in my young calligraphy business. In our small business, which offered a service that would eventually be rendered obsolete by computers, we enjoyed some significant successes, though they usually were hard-won and never could be depended upon to last. Gradually I became aware that I was not content. I wanted things – I wanted security and I wanted success.

Although I have been thinking about life and trying to "figure it out" for as long as I can remember, I officially became what we call a "journeyer" with the reading of *The Road Less Travelled* by M Scott Peck. My brother introduced the book to me by saying, "Read it; it will change your life." He had not exaggerated its value, nor had he been wrong about what it would mean to me. I loved it. I formed a book club around this amazing book, gathering women who enjoyed it as much as I did and wanted to discuss it. At our first meeting, we read the first line of the book and became engaged in a discussion about it. "Life is difficult," Peck wrote. Everyone in the book club experienced life as difficult in one way or another and we were all surprised we weren't alone in that feeling. We continued to discuss that line for months.

My frustration in my efforts to achieve success made life seem difficult to me. In my search for answers, I read many other self-help books. I listened to Earl Nightingale's *Lead the Field* and Anthony Robin's *Unlimited Power* on cassette tapes. In 2006 I ordered the DVD of *The Secret*. My daughter, who watched the movie with me that first time, took the concepts and ran with them – for her, they became increasingly clear and applicable to her life. Disappointingly, nothing seemed to change in my life.

So many of the success stories I read were about people who survived challenging childhoods and, despite this, soared to the tops of their fields. I began to wonder if having a turbulent childhood was the *key* to success. If that was the case, I was out of luck. My childhood was as close to perfect as you can imagine. I grew up in an upper-middle class family, the oldest of four children. My father was in partnership with his two brothers in a prosperous and growing business. My mother, like most mothers in those days, stayed at home. My parents had been married for forty-seven years when my mother died. There were no major problems in my childhood.

Yet here I was, as an adult, the only child who gave her parents cause for concern. My siblings did well for themselves as adults. They didn't struggle for money as I did. It seemed I was always unhappy about my business, always wondering why no matter what I tried I couldn't manifest this one dream – to be successful. Shouldn't I, after all these years, have figured out how? And why did my happiness rely so much on the self-worth I believed success would bring when everything else in my life was perfect? I had a wonderful husband, two amazing children, excellent health, many good friends, a close extended family and a beautiful home. I was blessed in every other way.

As the years passed, I discovered Hay House Radio online, where I was introduced to many great authors. I tried prayer and meditation. I learned how to use EFT (Emotional

Freedom Technique) and tap out my unwanted feelings; I fell in love with Byron Katie's "Work" and Donna Eden's energy medicine. I used the Sedona Method, learned some QiGong, and did Ho 'oponopono. I studied Quantum Touch and became a Reiki Master Healer with a passion for healing so strong that I gave most of my treatments away for free, but I could not heal my own unhappiness.

One Saturday morning, I was driving to my father's house to pick up his mail while he was out of town. I spotted a garage sale in his neighbourhood and pulled over. From where I was parked at the side of the road, I could see two tables inside the garage covered with books, so I went in to investigate.

They were more than just books; they were *my* kind of books – works by Neale Donald Walsh, Gary Zukav, Marianne Williamson and many more precious tomes I had borrowed from my favourite section of the library over the years! The husband of the woman who had owned the books explained that they were downsizing and this was why his wife was selling them. When I left I was carrying two plastic grocery bags bulging with books to my car.

I never saw the woman who had owned the books because she was inside the house during the sale, but she haunted me long me after I drove away. Not only had she bought the books that I loved, but she was now parting with them. What had she learned that enabled her to leave these books behind?

While she was relinquishing books, I was acquiring them as fast as I could. My appetite for reading was insatiable. As I approached my fiftieth birthday, I told my husband that I didn't want to go out for dinner. I wanted books instead. This decision added three more treasures to my library: a book by Doreen Virtue on Chakra clearing, *Happier Than God* by Neale Donald Walsh, and a book by the fellow who was featured in the movie "What the Bleep Do We Know," Joe Dispenza, called *Evolve Your Brain*.

I would come to refer to Dr. Dispenza as "my good friend Joe." His book on how the brain works combines chemistry, biology and quantum physics. I studied this thick, wonderful tome slowly over the next three months. I marvelled at the brilliance of it, told all my friends about the book, and carried on with my life.

Anthony de Mello once said at a workshop that he was conflicted by something he observed in his psychotherapy practice. He said that he feared he was merely helping people to find *relief* from their problems. This, he felt, only served as a soft place to fall and prevented the crash to the bottom that might have forced his clients to recognize what it was they were truly feeling and why. Perhaps this soft place was what these books provided for me. At first I would be elated and excited to share my new discovery with friends and family, but after a while I was still essentially where I had been before my revelation, only a little more discouraged than before.

I blamed myself. There must be something wrong with me. It seemed I had no commitment, no staying power, and no ability to hold the ground I had gained. I lost it, gradually, every single time. I recognized the fact that my feelings and moods changed in response to my environment. When our young Internet business generated income, I felt good; when business was slow, I felt bad. I was an emotional yo-yo. I *knew* this, but I didn't know what to do about it. I was running out of books. I was running out of time.

Sometimes many things in life conspire at once to bring us to the doorstep of our pain in order for us to learn the lesson we need to learn for the sake of our happiness. I don't believe we *cause* bad things to happen so that we can learn the lessons. Sometimes, though, the only way we can ever find that hidden treasure is if we are shipwrecked on the island where it is buried.

My life wasn't a shipwreck – yet – but I was getting ready to leave my safe harbour and go into new territory, both emotionally and physically. For seven years, my daughter and I had talked about the mother-daughter trip we would take "one year," and this was the year. I was going to Greece with my daughter!

3

Preparations

"...try to imagine it as an adventure,
all sorts of things might happen."
~The Railway Children~
E. Nesbit

Twenty-five years ago, I had taken a mother-daughter trip
with my mother to Europe. At that time we simply poured
over the travel brochures, went to her travel agent to book a
tour package and went home to wait for the departure date.
This trip would be very different. Natasha and I didn't want to
feel constrained by schedules. We wanted to experience the
Greek culture by mingling with the people rather than merely
observing them through the windows of a tour bus. This
meant no tour package and no tour guide. This meant
mapping out the trip ourselves and using the Internet to
research and book hotels and ferries. We would be on our
own. Even though my daughter was a mature twenty-three-
year-old adult, she had never experienced international
travel. I felt as if I would be in the driver's seat. The

responsibility sat heavily with me. To say I had some travel anxiety would be putting it mildly.

Two months before our departure, when all our plans had been painstakingly made and our hotels and ferries booked, riots broke out in Greece over economic policy. The country was in deep trouble and letting the world know it. My friends started asking if we were still planning to go ahead with our trip. I stayed calm, praying that all would be well by May 15th.

In mid-April, the Eyjafjallajökull volcano in Iceland erupted, unleashing an ash cloud that grounded air traffic in Europe indefinitely. My husband, watching the news closely, said that the last time this volcano erupted the ash cloud lingered for months! He warned that our trip would be precarious if it were possible at all, and suggested we consider cancelling.

Two weeks before our departure, we received a letter from a lawyer informing us that our next-door neighbour was threatening to sue us for nearly five thousand dollars. We knew his case was ungrounded but we also realized it would cost more money than we cared to spend if we had to hire a lawyer to help us prove it. I couldn't imagine leaving the country and enjoying my trip with Natasha while my husband was back home dealing with this. I was at the end of my rope, tying knots and hanging on for dear life.

It was at this time that I came across Joe Dispenza's radio program online. I started listening. Over and over again, I listened whenever I was at the computer, which was where I worked, no matter what I was doing. I needed to learn how to alter my brain so I could change myself and my life, and Dr. Joe was convincing me it was possible.

As I listened to Dr. Joe's program, one thing fired my imagination. He said he never gets out of bed in the morning until he has thought about how he would be if he were living "the highest ideal of Joe." I wondered what the highest ideal of Lori would be. What words would describe her?

I have always been intrigued by the idea that the world is created with words. Words described us when we were children. The words of adults formed our self-identity. Conclusions, prophecies – these were magical words. I understood what Joe was saying – I loved it and I ran with it. I knew that this time I could choose the words to recreate myself; I just had to discover the words that described who I wanted to be.

I went to work and immediately came up with five Words: Capable, Loving, Wise, Prosperous and Content.

I decided to do what Joe Dispenza does and spend extra time in bed in the morning reviewing my Words. Then I would get out of bed a new person, a Capable-Loving-Wise-Prosperous-Content person. Immediately, amazingly, just as he said, things in my world began to shift!

One morning I was inspired to write a vision of my ideal life that daily became clearer. I saw myself writing, healing, presenting.

This caused me to start thinking about writing again. Writing is something I have wanted to do from the moment I read my first Bobbsy Twins Mystery novel at the age of eight. Though my major in university was English and I had made several attempts to write through the years, the demands of raising a family and making a living left very little time and energy to write anything longer than a short story. I considered the idea of starting a blog just to get back into my writing. This idea was met with enthusiasm by friends, some of whom didn't even know it had been my lifelong dream to be a writer.

I loved doing Reiki energy healing work and I enjoyed doing presentations where I talked about energy work and the connection between the mind and the body. I began to envision myself presenting to large groups of people.

Then something unusual happened. Regularly I exchange Reiki treatments with my Reiki Master friend Dawn. While she was giving me a treatment a week before I left, she was inspired to share a message with me. Six words came to mind and she felt she had to tell me:

"Where you walk, you will remember."

We didn't know what it meant, but we felt intuitively it had to do with my fast-approaching trip to Greece. I was intrigued. *What would I remember?*

A week before our departure, in the middle of the weekend when we were celebrating a family wedding, my husband convinced our neighbour to drop the lawsuit. The riots in Greece momentarily quieted and the ash cloud drifted away from Europe. We breathed a sigh of relief and started to pack.

I was anxious to share with Natasha the unusual happenings of late, including the story of my "Words" and the mysterious message Dawn had shared that seemed to relate to our trip. But in all the excitement since she had arrived home and with all the last-minute things to do, we hadn't had a moment to talk.

May 15th dawned bright and clear. My husband drove us to the airport and waved good-bye as we went through security. We were sitting on a pseudo-padded bench waiting for the announcement to board and I turned to Natasha and said, "I have a story to tell you..."

With that, as if by magic, she became a part of the story. And her role in the story brought me to a place I never dreamed I would see.

Natasha Eve: a name that just sounded right to us when we lay in bed considering different names for our first child if the baby were a girl. We didn't know it then, but "Natasha" means "born on Christmas day" and "Eve" means "the mother of all living." She was both child and mother to me, especially there, in Greece. And there in Greece, she would help me give birth to a system for self-healing that would change my life.

4

Greece

"'What makes the desert beautiful,' said the little prince,
'is that it hides a well somewhere...'"
~ The Little Prince ~
Antoine de Saint-Exupéry

During those first few days as we excitedly explored Athens, I couldn't help but recall my trip to Europe with my mother twenty-five years before. I often found myself saying, "When *Sittie* and I were in Europe..." ["Sittie" is Arabic for Grandma]. Being in Europe again brought the memories flooding back to me. I apologized repeatedly for doing this, but Natasha said she didn't mind. She had been very close to my mother and loved to hear stories about her.

Natasha was the perfect traveling companion. She was calm, pleasant to be with and confident in gaining her bearings as we found our way around the different islands. Day after day as we dressed to go out, she raved about how wonderful I looked yet I dismissed these compliments with self-disparaging remarks. I didn't believe her praise to be any more than bolstering – something encouraging you said to "Mom."

How could anyone look good next to her? She was beautiful inside and out. I sometimes felt as if beauty skipped a generation – she and my mother enjoyed it, while I stood back and watched. The resemblance between them was striking. Natasha had the same way of smiling – the same high cheekbones, the same sultry glint in her eyes. Being with her in Europe was *déjà vu*, like having both my mother and my daughter with me. I could see my mother in her eyes, in her expression. I could see her in Natasha's love of life.

When the boys and men smiled at her, she smiled back. When they said, "You have a Greek face!" or "You will marry me!" she laughed with delight. Day after day, wherever we went, men doted on her and she accepted their compliments easily, loving it, celebrating. My heart should have been swelling with motherly pride, but I didn't feel that way.

It was halfway through our trip, on an evening when we were having supper in a *taverna* in Iraklion, Crete, when she asked me the question. She posed it tentatively, innocently, as only she could.

"When you were on your trip with *Sittie*, did she do what you do? *Did she put herself down?*

I felt as if my world ground to a halt. No. She... hadn't.... but Mom and I were closer in age, 22 years apart rather than 28. When we were in Europe, everyone thought we were sisters. I had wondered why everyone in Greece seemed to know Natasha and I were mother and daughter, but 23 and 51 is quite different from 25 and 47. No, Mom had never put herself down.

Why was I doing it?

Pandora's Box had been opened. The question had escaped. It waited while I slept, giving me merciful hours of oblivion before pouncing on me when I awoke. Then I experienced the first bad feeling I had in Greece. The question was sitting on my footboard and tapping its foot, waiting for me to provide an answer. Natasha was still asleep. I was lying in the twin bed adjacent to hers, hiding behind closed eyes. I would *not* get out of bed while I felt this way.

It was then that I remembered something else Dr. Joe had said: during the first few moments of your morning, your brain will lie to you. I had come to understand it in this way; upon awakening, your brain will reveal its agenda. The brain's agenda is to take care of you by giving you what you want. How does it know what you want? Easy. You have told it what you want by feeling the same feelings for so long that it has evolved to accommodate those feelings by creating more receptor sites on the cells to receive the chemicals created by these feelings. Your brain is wired to give you what you want because you have requested it so many times. Your body upon awakening will tell you which chemicals you lack – which feelings you have become addicted to and haven't had a "hit" of in a while. Once you have a feeling, you will find or manifest a reason for feeling that way, which will give your brain the chemical hit it has become accustomed to receiving. Thus the status quo is maintained.

I was all too familiar with those morning feelings, but things had shifted since the adoption of my Words; I had been waking up *feeling good.*

I knew I needed to name the emotion I was feeling so I could discover the source of the addiction. I recalled the *taverna* where we'd had supper last night and the waiter who had brought complimentary Ouzo and plates of sweet dessert to our table. When we left, the waiter had distractedly shaken my hand as I walked past him into the Greek evening. He then hugged Natasha, who followed me, holding her and gazing at her affectionately then kissing her on both cheeks. I had felt invisible.

This feeling showed in my eyes. I could see it in every photograph taken of me – *that look.* "That look" is in my eyes in a photograph hanging on my parents' wall in their basement. I was just four years old. The often-photographed, first-born child of a photographer, I always believed I wasn't lucky enough to possess the photogenic gene. Was that true? Or was it possible that the way I felt about myself and about life was being perfectly captured on film?

This feeling was about not being good enough, smart enough or capable enough. Yet it was deeper than that. It was about always taking second place to someone else. When I took ballet lessons at the age of eight, Madame said I was "very graceful" but I was not as good as Joan, the best dancer in the class. The best I ever did in cross-country races in high school was second place. In modeling, I was graceful and competent, but there was always someone more graceful, more beautiful – better than me. In junior high, I played center on the junior basketball team until my younger sister, who played center on the senior team, came to play with the junior team for the important games. She claimed my position and I moved down to second string center.

Second string. Sitting on the bench. This was beginning to capture how I felt. But *why* did I feel this way? Where did I get the idea that I would always be "second"? It did not originate at the age of eight. I knew it came before that. What had caused me to feel that way for the first time, and enough times after that, to wire it so firmly in my brain that I continued to crave the chemicals for that feeling

I started to examine my friendships and made a disturbing discovery. I don't consider myself to be as wise as Marie. I am not as good a healer as Dawn. I am not as prosperous as Stephanie. I am not as smart as Judy. I don't believe myself to be as peaceful as Marlene or as classy as Jocelyne, as poised as Leanne, as articulate as Amy, or as intelligent as Christine. In every relationship, I *lost* by comparison.

When my mother or father or an uncle said I was beautiful, I didn't believe them. I knew I wasn't beautiful; I could see the photos. Nor did I believe my daughter when she told me I was beautiful. *She* was beautiful! In comparison to Natasha even the most beautiful woman would question her own allure, and did – I observed them while they looked at her. I felt second, I felt defeated; I was relegated to the sidelines permanently. I was never quite *anything* enough.

These feelings caused me to keep score, to judge others in relation to myself – better or worse. I couldn't win unless someone else lost. If only in my mind, I had to find a way to make *them* lose because losing had become so painful *to me.*

This trip with my beautiful, much-loved daughter who celebrated life and the people in it had lured this issue out of the shadows and into the light for me. This situation was perfectly ordained. I would never have "gotten" it in any other situation or with any other person. She was my firstborn, heart of my heart! I was going to lose *this* battle because I was unwilling to make *her* lose so I could win.

I allowed these thoughts and feelings wash over me. Then came a moment of clarity and insight that caused me to catch my breath.

When I was fourteen months old, my sister was born and I became "Mommy's little helper." I helped my mother take care of her and the next two siblings who followed within the next four years. Everyone around me, except for the little siblings I cared for, was bigger, smarter, stronger, and more capable than me. I was second to everyone, particularly to the one I most looked up to: my beautiful, capable mother. I had become accustomed to feeling "second" to the person I admired most while I was still forming my identity, while I was still a very young child.

I knew I had to break the addiction to this feeling because it was manifesting my reality. I needed to create new connections in my brain. I needed to find the antidote feeling to add to my list of Words – the Word for what I wanted to experience and be for the rest of my life. *What was the word?*

It wasn't easy to find. I sampled many different words, but in the end it was two words that satisfied me: *Mighty Excellent.* I am not a perfect person, but a perfect me whose perfection is not challenged by anyone else's perfection. In light of, despite, no matter what, *after all this time* – I am Mighty Excellent after all!

It felt so right; I knew it was right. It felt as if I had turned on a light in a room that had been shrouded in darkness. The bad feeling immediately *dissipated.* I felt elated, dizzy with happiness. I knew that when I got out of bed it would be as a different person and that the world I would touch when I stepped onto the floor would be a completely different world.

I knew this in theory. The reality was about to surprise me.

That day we went to the Historical Museum in Iraklion, Crete and had lunch at a café on the waterfront. After that we stumbled upon the Old Bazaar and shopped. Then we purchased some fresh fruit and went back to our hotel to get out of the sun and rest for a while. I didn't say anything to Natasha about what had happened until that evening when we were sitting in another *taverna* near the waterfront having supper.

Her reaction floored me: *she had noticed!* She had felt a difference in me *all day.* She said I *looked* different. I no longer questioned her sincerity, because now it seemed I couldn't take a bad picture. I felt different inside *and it showed.*

Suddenly, as if you drew a line down the middle of our trip, people we met assumed we were sisters. I didn't have any reason to wonder if I was imagining this dramatic shift. The looks of surprise and disbelief on their faces and on Natasha's face as I corrected them was evidence enough that the whole world was responding to the changes I felt inside.

Then came the incident, several nights later, which proved beyond a doubt that the changes within me had made changes in my world. It was our last night in Perissa Beach, Santorini. We decided to return to the club where we'd developed a friendship with Adelphos, the owner, to say good-bye. We ordered a drink and Adelphos sat with us drinking coffee and smoking a cigarette. I asked him about the interesting and unusual trees that lined the road. He didn't know their name, so he motioned to a friend who was just arriving at the club. Stefanos, who appeared to be about halfway between Natasha's age and mine, stood next to our table making such a genuine effort to recall the name of the trees that I was becoming embarrassed I'd asked. Natasha thought he was "hot" so she invited him to take the fourth seat at our table.

For the next twenty minutes the four of us talked and laughed. The guys were teasing me because I was drinking a smoothie that Adelphos had graciously made for me. I knew Adelphos's cocktails included a generous amount of alcohol so I wasn't taking chances on his cocktails this evening, but I was taking a lot of ribbing. "I'm not a drinker," I finally protested, "I'm a dancer!" Immediately Stephanos seized upon this, suggesting we come to the club where he was working later, and dance. "We should all go!" he said. Natasha and I exchanged a look and remained noncommittal.

Then Stephanos had to go to work and Adelphos left to tend to some customers who had just arrived at the club. When it was just the two of us at the table again, Natasha leaned in and whispered, "Mom! Stephanos was into you! He tapped me on the shoulder as he walked behind me and whispered 'Get her to come!' He didn't even look at me!" I gazed in silence at the incredulous expression on her face with what I'm sure was a stunned look on mine. I hadn't even noticed!

Then I smiled, taking this in, thinking about how the tables had turned, at least for the moment, and enjoying it. I looked into my daughter's eyes and said, much in the way my mother would have, "Welcome to the first half of my trip!" And we both roared with laughter.

I knew I had fallen upon a system the moment I found my word that morning, May 24th, 2010. I was not to use the system again until I returned home. There and then, many issues presented themselves to be healed and, using the system, I healed every one. In the first two weeks, I cleared more life-long issues than I had in the past twenty years. The clearing of those issues made it possible for me to access and clear even more in the week and months that followed.

It was changing my life. It was changing me.

5

The Key

"Of course it is happening inside your head, Harry,
but why on earth should that mean that it is not real?"
~ Harry Potter and the Deathly Hallows ~
J.K. Rowling

I thought about what happened in Greece as I made the long journey home alone. Natasha had stayed in Athens, meeting a friend who flew in to travel with her for the next two months in Europe. In an eighteen-hour journey with no travelling companion, I had a lot of time to think.

At home, I faced challenges and I began to use the system that I dubbed "a Path to Peace" because peace was the destination. Every time I worked through an issue by following the steps on the Path, it brought more peace into my life. Again and again I was able to liberate myself from intolerable feelings. With each additional success I felt more in control of my life – more *me!*

I began to use the Path in my Reiki healing work with some of my clients. This created a need to explain it, which helped me to appreciate the beauty of it even more. I witnessed clients make significant breakthroughs by using this simple process. Life-long issues were being rooted out with amazing results. It wasn't just me – it could help other people, too!

I started talking about it to friends. I thought: *I have to write about this!*

Now that I had time to think about the system, I realized *why* it worked, why it all made such perfect sense. What I discovered was the missing piece in a personal theology for healing I had been slowly piecing together for a long, long time. In all my years of searching, I had only found the door. Now I was holding the key.

Welcome to the World

You've heard the stories of the babies in the orphanage who were fed and changed but never held, the ones who died? Science looks for physical explanations for that, but I have my own theory. They knew, even that young, that nobody really loved them, so they "left." I think we can come to conclusions when we are that young. I believe we all did. A Path to Peace led me to rediscover some incidents in my early childhood that were pivotal in forming the way I saw the world and constructing my strategy for survival.

I was a much-loved, highly anticipated first child of a young bride who lived fourteen hundred miles from the home where she grew up and where her parents still lived. She was twenty-one and living in the midst of her in-laws in a different country. I know she must have been homesick and a little lonely. The birth of her first child changed all that. I doubt there were many births celebrated more than mine or many babies more treasured. My father was a photographer and a photo finisher. I have the pictures to prove it.

I was a product of a loving home of the early sixties, including the culture, the environment and the parenting methods of the day. I was a child of Lebanese heritage, though both my parents were born in North America. This is only the outside picture of me, the template. It was what came after that which made me who I am.

Although I can't say I remember intellectually, I can piece it together well enough to know that all was well for the first year and two months of my life. That was when it happened – the event that changed my life in so many ways. It wasn't even a bad event; in fact, it was cause for a *second* celebration. My little sister was born.

The questions I had arrived in this life with – *is it safe here, is it OK for me to be here, is this a friendly place, who am I, how do I matter, what's my role* – had already been answered. Now I needed new answers because everything had changed. My role in the family had shifted. The amount of responsibility for my parents, both physically and financially, had increased. But worst of all, my parents' focus had turned away from me to the one who needed it more.

This was not a tragedy. This was *ordinary life,* but for me... for me it was cataclysmic. You may think it strange that it had affected me so profoundly. *You were just a child – a toddler!* That's the point. I wasn't able to understand why so much of the attention I had been accustomed to receiving was now going to this baby. I didn't understand where my mother had been for the past few days when she had been in the hospital, and I wasn't happy that my father was so excited about this baby.

My mother used to tell me the story. She said they sat me on the couch and put the baby on my lap, saying, "This is your baby!" She told me that sometime later that day I stomped my foot – something completely out of character for me. I don't remember my thoughts at the time, but based on the out-of-character foot-stomping and the things I have discovered during my time spent on the Path, I could guess they may have gone something like this: "I don't want a baby! Take it away! Why is everyone looking at her?"

I was a toddler getting only a glimpse of how my life was changing. I was interpreting events in my world to the best of my ability. I was making decisions about life that were becoming wired in my brain and I would live for many years believing the many conclusions I drew that day were truth. So little was understood about children in those days. They didn't understand how much children absorb from their environment and how they process the information. I watched. I concluded. I felt a myriad of feelings. And my brain recorded it all.

I didn't understand that for much of the time when I was very small my mother was pregnant; she was often sick and tired. I had no way of knowing that my father was busy with the young business he ran with his two older brothers which took up most of his time and that Mom needed my help. I didn't know my parents' stresses, their fears, and their problems. I just wanted them to take care of me.

When I was a teenager my grandmother used to look at me and say, "Ah Lori! She would prefer to have loved and lost than to never have loved at all!" I had been the centre of my parents' world. Now I was on the periphery. I had "lost" something substantial. My sister would never know what my world had been before she arrived in our family. She would never experience that kind of one-on-one attention. I had. I knew what it was to lose it.

My sister's arrival in my life changed the way I saw the world. Not only was there someone who stood between me and the immediate gratification of my needs, but now I was depended upon to be the helper. I had been the star and now I was playing a supporting role. This is not something an egotistical child takes well. I was a mild-mannered child, a "good girl." According to my mother, after stomping my foot that day I never again put up a fuss. It wasn't in my nature. It might have been better for me if I had a different nature, like my daughter.

When Natasha was twenty-three months old her brother was born, and he immediately needed surgery, which scared me to death. In the process of following the ambulance to the Children's Hospital in Halifax one-hundred and sixty miles away, meeting with the doctors and trying to nurse my baby as long as I could while attempting to hold myself together, I neglected my daughter. I wasn't callous; I just thought she was fine because she had her father with her. We were staying at my Aunt and Uncle's house, *together.* But this little girl's mother was miles away from her in spirit and she wasn't at all happy about that.

She tolerated this in silence for three days before she threw her first ever temper tantrum. There were two temper tantrums in two days and never another ever again after that. I got the message. I admired the messenger's determination to deliver it. She had only been wondering where her mother had gone. In some ancient part of me, I understood.

This is who I was. I didn't understand any of this until I stumbled upon the Path to Peace and began to recognize that I was living my life according to an out-dated, immature assessment of the world and of myself. I was operating on the premise that what I had concluded as a child was *reality*. Worse, I was acting as if the way I was treated in childhood was the way I'd *always* be treated. In a way, I was right. My expectations were creating my reality. They always do. I didn't know I had any power in creating the life I saw or with the way I saw myself. It all felt cast in stone, and it *was*. But it was cast by the hands of a child.

Much of my personal worldview formed around many of the thoughts, conclusions and feelings I had when I was only fourteen months old. It didn't stop there. That was only the place where it began.

Personal Worldview

Two more siblings followed my sister into the world. My brother was born when I was three and my baby sister when I was five. The birthdays of the last two were one and three days after mine, respectively. By the time I had blown out five candles on my birthday cake, I was one day away from being the oldest child with three younger siblings.

In later years when issues arose, I used logic to stomp them down. *How could I have anything to complain about?* We didn't struggle financially, physically, or in any other way! There was no verbal abuse or physical abuse in my childhood, and no alcohol or drugs. There was no neglect. I didn't understand then how subtle little incidents could have such formative affects. It was only when I started reading psychology books the summer I was twenty-one that I began to understand.

I was working at a daycare for children of underprivileged families that summer. The children ranged in age from two to five years old. Gradually I came to learn their stories from the senior staff members. The vast chasm between what I saw and what I heard was horrifying.

I would arrive at work in the morning to learn there had been a "crisis" the night before. Listening in disbelief, I would watch as a teacher pointed to a two-year-old playing in the sand box and tell me how he had witnessed a fight between his parents and saw his mother with a bloody nose, and that they had removed the mother and two children from the home. All I could see was a happy little boy, seemingly unaffected by what had happened, playing in the sand. His older sister angrily expressed her feelings about what she had seen. The boy would only do that later in life. Each one responded differently by either internalizing or expressing their anger, as was their nature. It was heart-breaking.

I learned a lot about parenting by reading psychology books. Seeing where things went wrong for people was like recognizing the potholes in the road. I could see that small things could have a huge impact because it was a small person who had to endure and make sense of them. I became hypersensitive to psychological issues, determining that when I became a parent, I would be capable of avoiding these potholes. I would be aware. But I didn't know then about the function of the brain, including how early it begins to process the world and how well it remembers.

Dr. Joe says that the brain catalogues everything. Everything we see, hear, feel and conclude goes into the computer and the brain prints out a template for life. By the time we have arrived at the age of reason, we have already made vital conclusions about ourselves, about the world and our place in it. The scary thing is that it is *a child* at the keyboard entering the data. That might be okay, if the child continually tweaked the program as he or she grew. That doesn't happen. We don't even know there *is* a program. We live our entire lives according to the perspective of life and of who we are that we formed when we were children. No one told us there was any other way to see it, any other way to live it.

Patterns

I have always had the unsettling feeling when things were going well that something "bad" was bound to happen. Could I have gotten this idea from the typical storyline in movies, books or television programs? Television programs and fairy tales made strong impressions on young minds – stories about heroes and monsters and dangers lurking in the darkness. As children still processing the world, we took everything in *without discriminating.* Books, television stories and movies all helped define my world as much as real-world events did, at a time when I was busy processing the data of my life that would complete my personal worldview.

My grandmother used to say, "Think positive!" I loved her for teaching me that. But for me, thinking positive was a magical game we played, something that worked sometimes and not at other times. I didn't understand it. I didn't believe I could change anything in my life because I didn't know how much power I'd had in creating my life in the first place. I created my life by default, and I was completely unaware and unqualified to do it, but I had done it and nobody could even tell me I had.

No one ever told us it could be different. What is Newton's law about an immovable object? He asserts, "Every object will remain at rest or in uniform motion in a straight line unless compelled to change its state by the action of an external force." Our *lives* are immovable objects! We carry on the way we have always carried on. We don't see our power to change our lives. But when it comes to other people's lives, well, that's a different story. We can see their patterns clearly. We can see what's wrong and would be able to tell *them* what to do, if they would only listen.

I believe everyone sees life in their own way, according to their experiences and their personal worldview. My friend and I could attend the same event and come away with completely different experiences of it. I would notice how friendly people were; she would notice those who didn't return her hello. My world was a happier world than hers. Afterwards, we could each use our experiences at the event to try to prove to the other (always unsuccessfully) that the world was the way we saw it and the other person was wrong.

In university, I noticed each of my friends seemed to be dealing with her own type of problem over and over again – dating the same type of guys and experiencing the same kind of heartbreak. One person would have one pattern and another person would have a completely different one, and they would each repeatedly experience their patterns. It got to the point where I knew what each friend's problem was before she even opened her mouth to tell me about it.

I wondered about my own problems back then, too. I didn't know why we had patterns or why I had the ones I did. Now I believe it has to do with our unique personal worldview. By the time we got to university, the patterns were in place; we had a lot of things figured out. Is my personal worldview accurate? Is yours? You bet they are. I can prove it to you and you can prove it to me. Our lives themselves are evidence that we got them right!

Who Am I?

Do you ever notice how you feel and act differently around different people? Around some people I am very witty (I love being around those people) and around others I am shy. I know when someone finds me intelligent because I have a marvellous vocabulary when I speak to them, but if I feel judged by someone, I tend to stumble over my words. I define myself by looking into the mirrors of the people around me. I have been doing it all my life.

They said I was a shy child, but I'm not sure I was. After a while I began to believe it, but later in life I was surprised to discover that I'm not shy! I was a "good girl," sure, setting an example for my younger siblings. I was responsible and hard working. I was paying attention. I knew when I got it right because I saw it in their eyes. That was the way it was for me growing up. I saw myself the way they saw me and I still see myself the way I did when I first looked into the mirrors of their eyes.

Inside, I essentially still feel the same way I felt as a child. We may look all grown up but we're still the same person we always were. In some ways we're still a bunch of kids playing Show and Tell, proving who we are and what we're worth and exclaiming, "Look at what I have, listen to what I've done."

I sometimes feel as if I am a child looking out through a window of adult eyes. When I first became a mom, I felt completely unqualified. When my daughter came to me for advice, I thought, "How can I give advice? How can I know what to say?" I may look all grown up, but the way I feel, deep inside, is still the same. I may play the mother role well, or the role of the entrepreneur convincingly, but I still have all those same feelings inside that I had when I was a child.

At times when I recognized this, as I did that day in Greece, I was shocked and dismayed. How could this be? How could I have lived my whole life so far not knowing that this underlying, unhealed wound was exerting such an influence on my life? It was as if my life had been hijacked by a child. It had. The child was the one who caused my brain to become wired the way it had.

I have become addicted to feeling the way I feel. I blame it on my brain. Sadness and many other feelings have produced their own chemicals in my brain, and it has gotten used to enjoying those chemicals. I am addicted to them! Is this why I can go only so long without these feelings rising in me again? Is this why the "knowing" is not enough to change me permanently? I think so.

I didn't see *my* role in creating the reality I have been experiencing because I formed my beliefs when I was so young that *I don't even remember doing it.* Why would I question reality? I have invested a lot of time in figuring how things work and they usually do work that way. Why mess with that?

I made vast assumptions about the whole world based on the little world I called home, and I didn't know I needed to review these conclusions before I left that home to make my own place in the world. That is unfortunate, and potentially tragic. Operating in adult life with a personal worldview created in childhood is like getting dressed in a business suit and trying to get to work on a tricycle.

Where was the template I needed to fix? Even if I could locate these defining incidents, I didn't know how to change them or why they had such a hold on me. Dr. Joe's book on the brain supplied the missing piece of the puzzle and the incidents in Iraklion that day put me on the path to solving it. I will be grateful for that trip to Greece for the rest of my life because it *gave* me the rest of my life!

I did the best I could under the circumstances. I survived my childhood, but I have been living my life according to a consensus made by a child. It is thus a faulty one, even though it was made during the best of childhoods.

The Path to Peace showed me the way to revise this consensus. It is so *simple!* I don't have to examine all of the beliefs that make up my personal worldview. I have found a way to recognize the errors in my personal worldview. They've been showing up in my life as problems.

How to Fix the Problem

The problems are not typical problems or even necessarily large problems. They have to do with how I feel about what's going on in my world. They are patterns of behaviour, annoyances, upsets and other disturbances in my life. Most of the time it seems I could make the problem go away permanently if I could only change the actions of the people around whom I feel the way I do.

Sometimes, I prefer to ignore the problem. Sometimes I try to fight my way through it. I have been doing it this way my entire life. But I am starting to see that if I continue to have the same problem over and over again, it's not the *problem* that is the problem – it's *me.*

I wish I could say that I've worked this out on my own, or even that I came to understand it by looking into my own life, but I didn't – not entirely. I see it all around me. It is always easier to see patterns in the lives of other people. I learned about this by watching how others live. Take John and Noah, for example.

John grew up in a family environment that was unable to satisfy his emotional needs. As a child, it seemed to him that no one even noticed he was alive. John resolved to do better when he became a parent. His son Noah therefore enjoyed the experience of having a very loving and attentive father. The two different childhood dynamics contributed to two completely different personal worldviews. This was why John and Noah had radically different experiences of the world. You could see this by watching what happened on a typical shopping trip.

No matter where Noah shopped, the response from the sales people was the same: respectful, patient, and accommodating. Noah had a soft voice and would pause to think before responding to a question. You might assume the sales staff would be impatient to be left standing there waiting for a young boy to make up his mind, but this was never the case. While he considered his question or response in silence, they stood patiently and waited; when he spoke in a soft voice, they leaned in to hear what he said.

They treated him like royalty. Why did Noah always receive such excellent service? Being treated this way was all he knew, and was therefore what he expected and tended to experience.

Contrast this to his father's conditioning during childhood to think that he needed to either speak loudly to be heard and demand attention, or contend with being ignored. John expected to have to fight for what he wanted, to be heard, and to be respected. He had done this for his entire life. Why would sales staff treat him any better than his parents had? He didn't think about these things, but they were there in the back of his mind. He would deny that he had the expectation of receiving bad service, but he was never surprised when he did.

It seems that the world is the way I expect it to be. I believe it is a friendly place, so that is usually what I find. I usually attract friendly people and find my way to friendly environments. In Greece, Natasha and I neatly avoided strikes and ash clouds that were still present. We flew from Paris to Athens in the morning, just before the ash cloud grounded all flights out of Paris that afternoon. We stayed one more day in Santorini because we serendipitously learned of a planned strike on the ferry service (before we went down to the ferry with packed bags) without disrupting our trip or costing us more. It was what we expected: a peaceful, happy trip. Life goes on around us – both the good and the bad – but we expected to experience the good and that's what we got.

I know there are many other realities out there, but I choose to live in mine. I try not to watch the news too often because I tend to absorb it and I know after a while that can change the way I see the world and my experience in it. They say the world has never had the number and type of problems it has today, but neither has it ever had the communication technology it has now. I guard how I feel. How I feel has too much creative power in my life for me to take it lightly.

I try to remember that the world I see is just the world *I* see. There's no point in trying to enforce my worldview on another. I know. *I've tried.* Everyone has his or her own way of seeing the world and you can't convince them otherwise. They don't want to accept mine any more than I will accept theirs. We are very guarded about our perception of what we view as our world. It's our personal reality. We don't let anyone tamper with that.

I don't think about what I believe any more than I think about how my car engine works. When it breaks down I think about it, though, and wish I understood what is beneath the hood. It is the same with my personal worldview. I am not concerned about my worldview until I have a problem in my life. It is then I want to understand it. I want to look under the hood and fix it. Pain is a powerful motivator. When I have a problem, I know there is something wrong with the way I see my life and myself. I know where to start. I start with me.

When my son was four years old, he dropped a pencil down the toilet. As my husband was fishing it out he said, "Alex, you're not supposed to put things in the toilet. You broke a rule. What do we do when someone breaks a rule?" Alex replied, "We *fix* the rule!" The personal worldview is *my* rule. I can fix it.

When my life presents more and more of the same painful experiences and I'm getting tired of them, when I have run as far as I can and pruned off as much as I can and changed myself as much as I can conceive of changing and it still hurts; when the pain in my life becomes intolerable, I know something has to give. My personal worldview is that something.

Could the personal worldview have *that much power* in determining the outcomes we experience in life? It does for me. Behind every intolerable feeling I couldn't make shut up or go away there was a belief, often one I was *completely unaware I had.* What held that idea in place? It turns out the culprit was my brain.

The Brain

In my brain there is wiring that reflects the emotions associated with the experiences I had when my brain was striving to make sense of my world. It is all recorded – all the experiences I had when I was a child, a toddler, a baby. In my brain are records of experiences I had while I was *in my crib.* All these experiences combined to produce my own unique view of reality.

Every time we have a new experience, there is a feeling associated with it, and with each feeling, a chemical is produced. We remember things more distinctly when there is an emotional content to the memory. I can remember exactly where I was and what I was doing when I heard about the airplanes crashing into the World Trade Center on September 11th, 2001.

Dispenza explains why it is that the more we feel certain emotions; the more the brain adapts to accommodate the chemicals associated with those emotions. As these cells divide, there are more cells in my brain ready to receive those chemicals associated with, say, anxiety, or joy, or sadness. My brain, accustomed to these chemicals, will require more and more of a "hit" of them over time. It is like any addiction – it takes a little more to reach the same level of intensity we had the first time we experienced a feeling. This explains why I usually feel what I usually feel. I have become addicted to feeling the way I feel most of the time. My brain will nudge me to manifest those feelings to keep the chemical balance called "me." It also explains why the problems get bigger over time, each one a worse version of the last. In a way, this is a blessing. Big problems are harder to ignore.

After dealing with many issues that awaited me when I got home from Greece, I noticed that life seemed to be presenting me with the issue that was most ready to be addressed or the pain whose time had come to heal. It was as if life was lining up my issues, prioritizing them, and organizing the incidents of my days so that I would address and heal the painful feelings in the best possible order, one by one. I felt guided, supported. There seemed to be some sort of intrinsic timing involved, a healing process with a beautiful will of its own.

Problems that were muted and dull before I had the tools to effectively deal with them seemed to come into focus now. I had become so good at "doing" my life that I no longer saw myself clearly. Who likes to upset the status quo? Not me! But when push comes to shove, *I'm* not going to be pushed over. I'll push back. When the problem would no longer retreat or shut up, when the feeling became intolerable, I seized it and stepped on a Path to Peace, not stopping until I had gone all the way to the end.

Too Close to the Fire

How do I find the beliefs formed in my past that are still affecting my life today? I see them in their perfect re-enactment in my present-day life. Again and again, I live through the same dramas. The people and places may change, but it is always me at the centre, feeling the same feelings I have always felt. Why does this keep happening? It happens because I am drawn to the familiar.

We seek the familiar, however precarious that unconscious decision, because *we know what to do* with the familiar. I imagine our cave-dwelling ancestors choosing a path in the forest. The logical, life-preserving action will be to choose the path that looks familiar because the unfamiliar path may be dangerous. Even if the known path has dangers, these are *known* dangers so the brain knows how to address them. We might not be so successful on the unfamiliar path.

Do you ever notice how your friends are strangely similar to your family members? Often my sister will say, "She's my Stacey [our other sister] friend," or "She's like you." My brother always described his new girlfriends as looking like or being like one of his sisters. In my unconscious desire for the familiar, I have attracted mothering friends, abusive friends, unhappy friends, negligent friends. I have friends who are just like my cousins, or my sisters or my brother. These people are like the ones who affected me in my childhood in a profound way either by kindness or injury; they were instrumental in helping me form my personal worldview. I don't do it on purpose, but surrounding myself with people who are like the people I grew up with gives me a chance to see what needs to be healed. It gives me another opportunity to heal it.

My father used to warn us that if we went too close to the fire we would get burned. Our lives are *lived* too close to the fire – the fire of our childhood pain. We try to run away from it, but again and again we run smack into situations that are similar to the ones we experienced as children. We are *attracted* by the warmth of the fire. We are getting burned all the time.

The attraction of the familiar smokes out the errors in my personal worldview so I can correct them. I hate problems! Even knowing that an intolerable feeling is an invitation down a path that will change my life, I still resist it with everything I've got. But when I finally stop resisting it and walk down the Path to Peace, the problem has led to enlightenment, relief and healing for me. Every single time.

Is healing my past *that* important? It is for me. Until I have healed my past, I know that I am living as if the present *were* the past. I'm stuck there. Until I am healed, I don't deal with the present at all. I may believe I am driving the vehicle I call my life, but it is a child who is at the wheel most of the time.

When I began to dust off the memories and evaluate them again as an adult, I was surprised at what I found. So many faulty beliefs were stored in the basement of my subconscious, preserved in the wiring in my brain. I was so unaware! The feelings that alerted me to these beliefs would not be ignored indefinitely. There is no point in trying to go over or under or around the painful feelings any longer. That never works for very long. The only way out is through.

The Path to Peace takes me through.

6

A Path to Peace

"It's hard to be brave,
when you're only a Very Small Animal."
~ Winnie-The-Pooh ~
A. A. Milne

Naming the Feeling

the first step on the path

It all started with the way I felt that evening in Greece.
Feelings are what bring us to a place where we are forced to
make a change in our lives. What are these elusive things
called feelings and why do they exert such a powerful
influence in our lives?

I believe we learned how to handle our feelings by watching
how our parents dealt with theirs. My parents were taught to
honour their parents' feelings and learned very little about
dealing with their own. I was born into a "rugged individual"

generation where men never cried and women cried in the privacy of the bedroom. I know my parents wanted me to be happy, but they could only teach me what they knew. They could not give me what they did not have to give. As parents, we play the children's game of "hot potato." Our parents receive the potato from their parents and pass it along to us, and then we pass it along so fast we don't notice what it is we deliver into the hands of our children.

My feelings are part of what makes me who I am. What if I ignore my feelings because they are not socially acceptable? What happens to who I am if I defer to the way others believe I should feel or if I am asked to ignore my feelings to comply with a request that doesn't feel right to me? What happens to my autonomy and my sense of who I am if I blame my feelings on the words and actions of others?

I remember being asked as a child to hug an older uncle whom I didn't know and didn't really want to hug. I was taught to be polite and respect my elders. I was instructed to obey those in authority, even when my feelings told me otherwise. I have been warned about the "green-eyed monster," against being greedy, impatient, or even not smiling enough. I developed finely attuned antennae to the feelings of my parents, my peers, my teachers and my boss – and yet often I was completely disconnected from *my own* feelings.

I know it was not what anyone intended for me, but this kind of conditioning encouraged me to ignore my natural feelings. When I would feel something I thought I *shouldn't* feel I would judge it, feel guilty about it and stuff it away. I gauged my response to situations by what I thought I *should* feel. When I started down the Path to Peace, I was so surprised to discover the intensity of feelings buried long ago.

As an adult, I read books about how to release my unwanted feelings. Effective methods for doing this abound. I wanted to feel happy, which meant ridding myself of these unwanted feelings, but I wondered how sensible it was to release a feeling without first understanding it. It's like cutting off a weed at its stem. The root is still in the ground. The weed is going to pop up again eventually. In releasing my unwanted feelings without understanding them, I was rejecting the healing opportunity they offered. My intolerable feelings were coming from the "complaint department" of my soul, like little Natasha throwing a temper tantrum, letting me know that something was wrong. I needed to respect and honour this voice, not silence it. I needed to listen.

Ignoring my unwanted feelings didn't make them go away, though at times I believed it did because I had pushed them so far out of my awareness I had forgotten about them. Now I believe my brain had never taken its awareness from my problems even though I had convinced myself to not see them anymore. I had gotten pretty good at tucking my unwanted feelings away, but my brain remembered where I hid them.

Make Them Go Away

The feelings that nudged me to the Path were not all that serious, but they were real and *they hurt.* Over time they became intolerable. Some were so muted or "minor" that I felt guilty even talking to a friend about them, but they exerted a force in my life that was potentially crippling. The Path to Peace helped me deal with the ordinary, unwanted feelings that cast a shadow on my life.

I don't think the Path could help with the grief that comes from losing a loved one. Grief is part of a healing process that is logical and, within reason, has to be allowed to run its course. I do not recommend the Path for dealing with feelings associated with tragedy, illness, physical abuse or other kinds of crisis. Serious problems may require the assistance of a professional psychologist or psychiatrist trained in many different systems of healing.

This is a tool for the lay people – you and I –people leading ordinary lives who want to lead extraordinary ones. People who like to figure things out for themselves, who are tired of being frustrated by repeatedly experiencing the same problems in their lives.

I didn't try to banish every unwanted feeling at once. There was a much simpler, saner way, one perfectly tailored *to me.* I stepped on the Path to Peace when I experienced one of these types of key feelings:

1) An unexplained "down," "off" or disturbed feeling upon awakening in the morning that seemed to be there before I had even had time to think. This was the feeling I experienced that morning in Greece.

2) An emerging pattern: when I found myself wondering why I always felt a certain way, such as jealous, for instance, or frustrated, angry, or sad. Sometimes it was a new pattern that I recognized after it had occurred just two or more times. At times it was an all-pervasive, feeling-less feeling; it was like feeling nothing at all.

Interestingly, the "pattern" was also part of my Greek adventure. I had always felt "second" to my friends, but I hadn't *noticed* the pattern. The feeling was flying under the radar. Rather than being intolerable, it had become normal to me because I had been living with the pattern for so long.

3) An over-reaction in which I would see and hear myself and could feel that my response was "over the top." It would catch me by surprise and I did not know why I responded as I did.

4) A bad feeling resulting from something that happened that stayed with me for many days. This could be a feeling of embarrassment or regret.

5) An out-of-sync response, differing slightly from an overreaction in that it could be a quiet response. I would find myself feeling upset about something that I believe should not have bothered me. I could not seem to let it go. I may have been especially irritated at someone or bothered by something that happened. I knew when I had had an out-of-sync response because it just felt slightly "off" from what I expected I should feel.

Here, too, life was tapping me on the shoulder in Greece. I knew I should have felt proud at all the attention Natasha was receiving on our trip. I didn't feel proud, though. I noticed this, but this feeling was not enough to make me stop and question it. Sometimes I would experience many of these key feelings before I noticed that something was wrong.

Ultimately, I decided whether or not an unwanted feeling was one that should inspire a walk down the Path. The key feelings usually didn't get my attention until they had been around for a while – until they had become intolerable.

I never had to search for unwanted feelings to heal. They found me. When I experienced one of the key feelings, even before that feeling became intolerable, I started down the

Path, beginning with the first step. I asked myself, *how do I feel?*

I attempted to capture the emotion with a word. Sound easy? It's not as easy as you might think. Sometimes this step took a long time. When I was having difficulty naming the feeling, I would get a piece of paper and write whatever came to mind or I'd go to a keyboard and type. Ranting about the feeling to a friend, or even aloud in an empty room, helped me to identify it.

This was challenging because I was trying to name a feeling that had become "normal" to me. I'd gotten used to ignoring that feeling. Sometimes it was hidden beneath other feelings. For instance, many feelings are masked as anger. To see what was beneath a surface feeling and get to the deeper meaning of how I felt, I would use questions as I did for a client who was feeling angry:

"What do you feel?"

"Anger."

"Why? What is the anger about?"

"I feel as if my husband doesn't help me enough – I don't feel supported by him."

"What would 'anger' want to say if it could speak?"

"It would say, 'I'm TIRED of this!'"

"Why would it say that?"

"Because I'm tired of carrying all the weight!"

"'Carrying all the weight': what does that mean?"

"It means I have no support. I shoulder all the worry myself."

"How does it feel to shoulder the worry?"

"It feels heavy."

"How does 'heavy' feel?"

"It feels scary."

"How does 'scary' feel?"

"It feels alone – I feel alone!"

Bingo. There was a big difference between "angry" and "alone." "Alone" gave her the "Aha!" feeling.

I continued asking myself questions like this until I found a word that described the feeling so well I could sense it in my body. When I found my word, I would say it in a sentence in my head or aloud, beginning with "I feel..." If I sensed it in my body, I knew I had named the feeling correctly.

Sometimes I knew the word I found would not make sense to anyone but me. I didn't care. Each of us has a personal relationship with words. As long as the word "spoke" to me, I knew I was on the right path.

Where's My Autonomy?

One of the many issues I have dealt with so far has had to do with autonomy. I will share here how I walked with it down the Path, beginning with naming the feeling.

The issue: As this manuscript got to the point where I considered publishing it, I realized I had a problem. I *thought* my book was good, but I couldn't be sure. This horrible feeling of self-doubt, fear, and uncertainty was not new – it was a familiar pattern – but it was becoming intolerable because I no longer wanted to *be* this way! I decided to take the feeling down the Path.

What do I feel? As I thought about it, I realized it all boiled down to one emotion: the feeling that I couldn't trust my own judgment. I never knew whether something I did was good or not. I quietly deferred to others, looking for their affirmation in order to feel good about my decisions. I realized I had no autonomy. This statement, "I have no autonomy," was my starting place. It named a *thought* but it didn't capture the feeling for me. It was an intellectual statement, not an emotional one. I didn't feel it in my body, either.

I dug deeper. *What did I really feel;* what was the deeper emotion? It took some time for me to identify it, perhaps because I didn't want to face it. It finally, it came to me: "I feel incapable." This perfectly expressed how I was feeling about myself in this situation. I could feel it in my body; it was there in my chest and in my throat.

Finding the Origin of the Feeling

the second step

Once I had named the unwanted feeling, I took the next step: I followed it home. The feeling never lived in the present, except in my memory. My destination was the past, my childhood, where most of my ideas about life were formed. I realized that even though what I was feeling seemed to be in response to what was happening in the present, it had very little to do with the present. What I was responding to was a re-enactment of a childhood issue I needed to heal. I had felt this feeling before. I had been involved in this type of dynamic *a long time ago.* Only this time, however, I could heal the hurt because now I had wisdom, maturity, experience and knowledge that I didn't have when I was a child. Now I had a system!

Why do we keep feeling the same painful feelings? On the night in Greece when Natasha asked me the question, we played cards after supper as we often did in the evenings. I was losing and for some reason I was really bothered by it. I don't ever enjoy losing but I usually managed to completely ignore the part of me that was competitive. Not this time. I felt anger welling up inside me. I was *tired* of losing! The feeling that was becoming intolerable for me was even being expressed through a simple game of cards.

I wasn't upset because I was coming second in a game of cards; I was coming second in a game of cards because I was upset about *feeling* second and it was time to heal this part of who I was. I was a competitive person because I didn't want to feel second. Everything, even losing in a game of Rummy 500, was a manifestation of my personal worldview!

Wait, you ask, wasn't Natasha winning? What does that say about *her?* Since we played cards often, we took turns winning and losing but this wasn't an issue for her. Losing at cards did not reopen a corresponding emotional wound for her because *there was no wound to open.* As long as I was winning I was able to remain oblivious to the fact that I felt "second." Before that night, losing hadn't really bothered me. It bothered me that night because many recent events had combined to impact an old wound. They had resulted in a persistent painful feeling I could no longer ignore.

Those feelings were the true feelings I had about life and about myself. They were the unhealed emotions tangled up in misunderstood and painful episodes of my past. To understand why I felt this way I needed to go back to the original painful event, to take a second look. I needed to return to my childhood once again.

When Was the First Time I Felt this Way?

I would go back to the past because I left something of value there. I left a part of *me.* It was lost to me because I didn't understand what was going on and I drew conclusions that have negatively impacted my life. I would go back to my childhood to find the truth.

It might seem strange that I would return to a painful place in my past. Going back to a painful memory is a little like looking under the bed to confirm that there really weren't any monsters. I wanted to see what happened in order to understand how I processed it and know why it affected me the way it had. I would go back to understand it from the perspective of an adult rather than the perspective of a child.

Often I found myself coming upon feelings that had been hidden from my awareness for many years. I was surprised to discover a wellspring of emotion relating to the memories I found. The little child who was hurt still lived inside me. The strength and depth of the emotions often rocked me to my core. At times I would find myself on a downward spiral of despair.

I know intellectually that very little of what happened to me in my childhood was *because* of me. Very little of what anyone does at any age is about anyone other than themselves. It wasn't about me, but I thought it was. On this step of the Path, I tried to disengage from what happened. As a child, I had painted a part of my self-portrait as a result of occurrences of which I had limited understanding but for which I took responsibility. I allowed what happened to define me, and what defined me shaped my life because it immediately became hard-wired into my brain.

Sometimes I would get swallowed up by those old familiar feelings. The feelings were as real in the present as they had been in the past. Sometimes I would curl up in a ball and cry. I would have to *remind* myself to keep moving down the Path to the next step because coming upon an old wound, still raw, was often paralyzing. But I would remember my process and keep moving.

After I had been flattening the grass on the Path for several months, I was able to clear issues faster and faster. All I needed to do was say; *Step 1 - What am I feeling; Step 2 - When did I first feel this way,* etc. I got better at remembering not to let myself get stuck at Step 2. I got better at accepting what I discovered and moving on. I didn't want to hurt anymore. I wanted to keep going so I could find peace at the end of the Path.

What Can I Trust?

In trying to understand what happened in Greece, I read more psychology books, and in the process I learned some surprising things about memory. Modern psychological studies tell us we can't trust our memories. Sometimes we overlap memories, we overwrite them, we fill in gaps and we confuse them. Sometimes in memory too many things get lumped together.

Before I married, I dated a fellow who had a long and noticeable scar on his chest. When my younger cousins were visiting one day, he went outside and played basketball with them in the driveway. When I looked out the window I noticed that as they wrestled for the ball the boys were both climbing on his back. A few years later, when I saw my cousins, I asked them if they remembered my friend who had played basketball with them that day. They remembered, they said; he was the fellow *with the scar on his back.* They had retained two significant aspects of that day: the scar on his chest and climbing on his back to wrestle. It seemed these two aspects had gotten confused in their memories.

The only part of the past I know is "real" is my *interpretation* of what happened. That interpretation is contained in my memory, stored in the wiring in my brain and expressed by the feeling that I follow home.

I can trust my feelings. I just need to remember that my feelings are *based on my interpretation* of what happened. I trust them, but that doesn't mean the "tale" they tell is reality. It is only the reality of the child that brought down the verdict on what happened.

I see it as simple math: A + B = C.

A: something happened

+ B: I interpreted it in this way

= C: it affected me in this way (the feeling)

My goal was to change C, the way it's affecting me today, by looking more closely at what happened (A) and how I interpreted it (B).

Whatever happened, happened. Whether or not I remembered it accurately, it didn't have to keep on happening. I could *change* that. I could look again, see it clearly and understand it in a way I never could before.

I can only see my life through the lenses of my personal worldview. Everything is coloured by my lenses, and the events are made brighter or dimmer by my perspective. I believe what I see is reality, but everyone else in my world believes what they see is reality, too. We are each looking out at the world through our own lenses and we are each seeing something different. The sad fact is that until we heal distortions in our personal worldview, we are still seeing the world in the way we saw it when we were children. As a child, I saw the world from a childish perspective but I'm changing that. In the process, I am going to craft it the way I want it because whatever reality I (re)create will be the one in which I live. If I can choose, I will choose the happiest one I can imagine. I don't need to stay in the world my childhood self created for me. She did her best, but it is time for the adult me to take over.

Most people don't even know they are still little children in adult bodies – I didn't. They don't realize that their view of the world is determining their experiences, and that it doesn't have to be that way! Consider my friend Cameron. He had a very painful childhood, with "disappointment" being the dominating feeling in his personal worldview. His parents had disappointed him by making promises and then breaking them. At a very young age, Cameron came to the conclusion that he should not expect anything from anyone because he was a person for whom promises would always be broken by the people closest to him. In the decision to not believe promises, he would not expect anything from anyone and he would not have to experience the feeling of being disappointed.

But it is too painful to go through life feeling this way, refusing to expect anything from those closest to you. In the human spirit is a propensity for wholeness that seeks to heal our pains even when we are unaware of them. In his life, Cameron was placed in situations again and again that would test his belief. Each new experience only affirmed what he believed but no longer wanted to feel: that life and the people in it would always disappoint him. You could argue with him that things could be different, since what he experienced was a manifestation of his own beliefs, but Cameron saw it as something outside of his power and he would defend his view that life was disappointing. After all, he had so much evidence that it was. He was so trapped in his worldview that he couldn't see that other people's lives were different.

When my personal worldview becomes something I defend rather than examine, I am trapped in it. Until my Greek adventure, I didn't even see the bars on my own cage. I would look beyond them into the cages of my friends, wondering why *they* didn't realize they were trapped. Why couldn't they see that their patterns, the problems they have repeatedly, are theirs and theirs alone? Why didn't they know they were the ones who were creating them? Why didn't I?

I have now found a way out of my cage. My feelings lead me. I started to look closely at the way I see life, examining one painful feeling at a time. With each key feeling I followed back to my childhood, I saw what I had based my conclusions on and decided if the conclusions I made as a child were still valid. I may have made mistakes. I may have gotten it wrong when I was only a few years old, but that's okay, because it is not too late to make it right.

You may be wondering if my key feelings all originated in childhood. Couldn't something in adolescence or other times in life have had such an effect? I have noticed that what I experienced in adolescence or later in life was an *effect* of the way my brain had become wired rather than an original cause for what I was feeling; the more recent events were symptoms rather than causes. If I first discovered a recent event to account for my key feeling, I would go back farther and farther into my memory, looking for earlier incidents as the true causes – as far back as memory would take me.

At rare times, despite intense soul searching, I couldn't locate the origin of the feeling. Maybe it was because the incident happened so early in my life that I couldn't access the memory. At other times, I recalled stories my mother told and filled in the blank spaces. But when I couldn't locate the origin of the feeling, I would just use the evidence of my present-day feeling to acknowledge that *something* had happened to cause my brain to be wired that way. I would let it go and move on to the next step.

When I discovered the origin of the intolerable feeling, I was always a little shaken, a little sad. It was like seeing the reveal of a movie, the climax of the story. It was temporarily paralyzing to come upon the scene from my childhood responsible for what I was feeling today. There was a quiet "Aha!" feeling. Sometimes there was a feeling of relief, but above all, there was a sense of discovery.

I would remind myself that the past is gone and the wiring in my brain was *all that remained.* I survived. Now I knew why I had seen my life in the way I had, and why it was so hard to see it in any other way. I finally understood my feelings around the issue. It made *sense.* For the first time, I could see it clearly. What did I do then? I moved on to the next step. I simply walked away.

Why I Lost My Autonomy

I had found the "I feel incapable" statement that described my unwanted feeling of lacking autonomy, so I moved to the next step: finding the origin, or that place in the past where this feeling was born. When had I felt this way before?

This question led me to two memories, both incidents occurring when I was five or six years old. The first incident took place when my sister and I were sitting at a little table coloring in our coloring books. Two adults were watching us. I was using a circular motion to fill in the lines of my picture, coloring with my crayon in happy little spirals, when someone leaned over and said, "Do it like your sister is doing it." I looked over at my little sister's coloring book and saw she had heavily outlined the part she was coloring and then was filling in the outlines with straight, light, even lines. My sister was fourteen months younger than me. "Do it like your sister is doing it"?! I took so many messages from that, not the least of which was: I don't know how to do things! I had been happy with the way I was doing it until I learned I had been doing it *wrong.*

The second incident occurred when I was in Grade One. I was coming in from an outdoor recess one day when I spotted some very important-looking papers in the large garbage can outside. I fished them out, brought them back to my class and proudly presented them to my teacher, who scolded me in front of the entire class for picking up "garbage" and bringing it inside. She told me to take them back outside and throw them away even though there was a garbage can right there at our feet! I can still remember that horrible feeling of shame I felt as I left the class and made my way to the garbage can outside.

As a result of these events, and likely more forgotten incidents that predated them, I had gradually come to the conclusion that I couldn't trust myself to know what to do. What seemed like a good idea to me often turned out to be the wrong thing to do. I began to look to others for guidance and affirmation. Everyone seemed to know better than I what to do. Only now I knew where this idea originated and I understood that it had caused my brain to be wired this way that was continually creating my experiences.

Choosing a Better Feeling

the third step

I always felt a measure of relief when I discovered why I felt the way I felt and why that feeling was so intense. That's the 90%; awareness. But the problem was, *I still felt the same.* I understood why I had always felt second while still feeling that way. I needed a way to step away from that feeling so that "always-second Lori" would stop running my life.

This is where the "knowing" falls short. Knowing never changed me enough and it never changed me permanently. I had taken those first two steps *for years!* I would discover why I felt a certain way and feel better – for a while. I never understood why I always eventually went back to feeling the same old feelings, but I know now. My brain hadn't changed. It was still wired the way it was before my revelation.

Understanding how the brain works made all the difference. It was because of this I was able to go beyond the second step in Greece.

At this step on the Path I asked myself the question that cuts to the chase. This is the game changer: *How do I want to feel?* I could change my life by changing the wiring in my brain. I would achieve that by changing my Words.

Words

I am intrigued with words. I think our worlds are formed with words, and our self-image is composed of words we heard when we were very young. Conclusions about me and about my world are all represented by words. I may have first heard the words from someone else, but once I accepted them, they became *my* words. The fact that my words may be unconscious in no way weakens their creative power in my life. My words are the building blocks of my identity; they are my personal appraisal of my worth.

When I chose "Mighty Excellent" in Greece, I began immediately to change the wiring in my brain. I have done it many times since returning from Greece, changing the wiring in the same way I created the wiring as a child by using words that represented feelings. I have made new connections that became hard-wired due to frequent use and allowed the old connections to atrophy from disuse. In this step on the Path I recreated – consciously, deliberately, and armed with my experience, knowledge, and adult understanding –what I did when I was a child. I could do it again. I could use different *words charged with feelings* to improve my life.

How did I *want* to see myself? How did I want to *feel?* I searched for a Word that made me feel *wonderful.* I tried different Words to see which one felt right. I knew it was important that it feel right. As I tried different words, I checked to see if I felt each one in my body in the same place I felt the unwanted feeling. That's how I knew when I found the right one. When I found the right word, it would bring another "Aha!" feeling; it brought about a state of mind that felt like coming home.

There didn't seem to be any rule about which bad-feeling words went with which empowering Words. Sometimes I started with a word opposite in meaning to my unwanted feeling, but that was just a starting place. The opposite word wasn't necessarily the one which worked best.

When I believed I had the right Word I said it aloud, beginning with the words, "I am." If I felt it in my body, I knew it was the right one. The feeling had filled the place where the intolerable feeling had resided. It had already chased the painful feeling away.

Re-Wiring My Brain

Once I discovered and claimed my Word, I substituted it any time I felt the old feeling. For instance, if my unwanted feeling was "I am second" and I began to feel that old response, I would interrupt my brain's tendency to connect with that idea and I would say, "I am Mighty Excellent." I did this again and again, as often as the old feeling arose. I knew my only antagonist was old wiring in my brain, which I was changing with my Words.

Did I *forget* that I am Mighty Excellent? Sure I did. That old feeling arising was just my brain's persistent and last-ditch attempts to do what it has always done – remind me to ask for what I have been asking for all my life. I would remind my brain that *I'm* the one in charge; I am Mighty Excellent *because I choose to be.* This wasn't a struggle. There was nothing to fight. I was just finishing what I started. I was deciding this time who I wanted to be. If my brain forgot, I reminded it. The less I plugged into my old intolerable feeling of being "second," the more that connection atrophied; the more I plugged into Mighty Excellent, the more that connection became hard-wired.

All I needed to do was interrupt the old connection and remind myself of my Word. My Words were defining me, one Word at a time. My Path to Peace is decorated with signposts of Words that deliver me to the places I want to be. Word by Word, I was changing my personal worldview. As I changed who I perceived myself to be, I began to see the world in a new way. When the way I saw the world changed, my life changed, too.

If an issue arose that was similar to one I had already cleared and had a Word for, I would just go to Step 1 with that feeling. Sometimes I would clear one facet of the episode only to discover there were others. I noticed that sometimes I had drawn many conclusions from one incident in my childhood, and each one was represented by a feeling. It seemed that some big issues needed many Words to address them fully. At times I arrived at a Word that represented a significant breakthrough and then, in looking back through my Words, I noticed that many that preceded it were harbingers of this Word.

Dealing with my unwanted feelings in this way was like watching a sculptor chipping away the parts that don't belong to discover the beauty that lies within the stone. Word by Word, I cleared away the debris from my past so I could remember who I really am. There was no battle to fight. Once I found my Word, it was time to leave the battlefield. It was time to go home.

Re-Claiming My Autonomy

Now that I knew why I saw myself as a person without personal autonomy and now that I understood why I felt fear and self-doubt and caution at times in my life when I had to make a decision, I was ready to choose my new Word. The Word for the direct opposite of feeling I had no autonomy was clearly "autonomous," but that had no affect on me. I needed a Word that would radically counteract that lack of personal autonomy I had been feeling for most of my life. What could make me feel *that* good?

Finally I landed upon a Word that would change my life. I would say, "I decide," or "I am the one who decides." I could feel that in my chest and my throat. My body affirmed that I had found my Word.

Integrating the Words

the fourth step

If I had done nothing more about it when I returned from Greece, "Mighty Excellent" would have been an inscription scribbled at the bottom of a photo from my trip and forgotten. I wanted to be Mighty Excellent at home. I intended to be Mighty Excellent *for the rest of my life.* So I wrote my Word in a small ringed notebook and I reviewed it day and night to integrate it. I felt pretty good at that point. I felt like a new me.

After a while more issues arose, and as I walked the Path to discover more Words I claimed them in the same way. Soon I had more Words in my notebook than I could hold in memory because issues were coming at me at a brisk pace. Sometimes I would try to dodge and duck the issues, but eventually, each issue had a walk down the Path with me. I continued to add the new Words to my notebook and watched as my life continued to change.

The temptation to stop once I found my Word was strong. At times I had such an overwhelming feeling of relief and joy when I found a new Word that I believed the transformation was complete. I was fortunate that Life kept me on the Path. If I hadn't been using the Path in my healing work, I might have become lax in the integration of my Words. If I hadn't needed to explain it to my clients, I might not have understood it as well as I came to understand it. We teach what we need to learn. I taught and – *oh boy* – I learned.

In the past, my process had ended once I arrived at the understanding of why I had felt the way I had. That had proven to be ineffective in making lasting changes in me. Now I understood that discovering the insight had only temporarily interrupted the wiring in my brain, but those old connections were strong and the new ones were too weak to replace them.

They say it takes twenty-one days to make or break a habit. In integrating my new Words, I was breaking a habit, the old wiring, and instituting a new wiring with my new Word. I decided to put a tally mark in my notebook for each day that passed in which I reviewed my Words.

Pillow Work

I developed a simple way of integrating my Words that kept me on track. I call it "Pillow Work." As I adopted a new Word, I wrote it down in my notebook on a page of its own, beginning with "I am..." and dated the page. Beneath the Word, I wrote briefly about the unwanted feeling that had given birth to it. Then I closed the notebook and put it on my pillow.

At night when I went to bed, I would open the notebook and do what I call the "Flip Flop Exercise." This exercise seemed to reduce any resistance I had to accepting my Words. Here are the steps for the Flip Flop Exercise, using my autonomy issue as an example:

1) Make the empowering statement: "I am the Decider."

2) Flip it over: "I never really **felt** as if I could decide on my own..."

3) Flop it back: "But **actually,** I really **am** capable of knowing what to do. I **am** the Decider!"

I did this for each Word in my notebook. This exercise was like a workout for my brain! I imagined my brain saying, "Wait! *What?*" It took seconds to do, but the way I felt when I did it was amazing! I would add the tally mark, leave the notebook on my nightstand and go to sleep.

In his classic work, *The Power of Your Subconscious Mind,* Dr. Joseph Murphy suggests that reviewing positive concepts before going to sleep is a powerful way to impress the subconscious mind. It gives the subconscious mind something to work on all night long while we sleep. To augment the integration process, sometimes as I slipped into sleep I would visualize my perfect life as this new Mighty Excellent person.

In the morning I opened the notebook and reviewed my Words, reminding myself who it was who was stepping into this new day. Then I returned the notebook to my pillow, where it would remind me to do the Pillow Work again at the end of the day.

I did this for at least twenty-one days for each new Word. I found that my addiction to the old feeling remained until I had completely accepted the new feeling and had hard-wired the new connections in my brain.

I kept a journal to help me see things more clearly. I paid attention to how my life was changing as a result of my time spent on the Path to Peace. Recording these changes kept me focused on the outcome I wanted, and focusing on the things I wanted to be, do and feel helped me to notice more and more of it in my life.

When the old feelings arose, I took note that this was my brain still operating according to my old instructions. I would say, "No, not that but this," and use the Word that applied. In the case of my issue with autonomy, I would think, "Not incapable, *I'm* the Decider!" I imagined myself unplugging cords from one area in my brain and plugging them in at another place. I did this calmly and consistently, as a mother does when she removes her child's hand from the buttons of the television. I didn't use anger or determination. I just reminded myself of how I chose to be.

Sometimes I adopted an attitude to help me integrate my new Word when I felt the old feeling. Rather than merely saying, "No, I am the Decider," I assumed the persona of a rap artist or a teenager and think instead with a wagging finger, "Oh, no you don't! We don't roll that way anymore – I'm the one who decides, Honey, so just get used to it."

From time to time I re-watched the movie *What the Bleep do We Know*. It has wonderful animations of the brain's functioning. It gave me a visual for the workings of the brain that I was in the process of rewiring.

Baby Steps

"I always tell my clients,
'Your past may have shaped who you are
but you decide who you want to be.'"
– Jillian Ross Hebb, Addiction Counsellor

A Path to Peace worked on one feeling at a time. I didn't have to wonder what issue to deal with next. There were no schedules I needed to follow. It was perfectly customized to me – my life, my hurts, my present-day dramas. I simply paid attention to the key feelings. When one arose and wouldn't go away, I knew it was time to start down the Path.

I knew I could rewire my brain because I had done it before. In the past, as a very young child, I formed my sense of self and my world by the faith I placed in the words with which I defined the world and my place within it. By walking down the Path I was doing it again, but this time I was doing it deliberately and consciously. I was changing my life by changing my attitudes, by changing my expectations, by changing my beliefs. I was doing it by eradicating one intolerable feeling, one step at a time.

An intolerable feeling nearly always led me to an erroneous belief about myself and, by extension, about my world. The unwanted feeling was the first bread crumb on the trail I followed. With a growing awareness of my power to make decisions, I followed this process to reach peace.

I celebrated the adoption of each new Word. I took it to work with me, wrote it on a piece of paper and taped it to my computer monitor. I wrote it with window markers on my bathroom mirror. Each new wonderful Word was worthy of celebration! Each new Word is a part of who I really am.

Evidence of My Autonomy!

Months after I adopted "Decider," I received affirmation that I had fully integrated this new wiring in my brain. After showing my manuscript to 27 people, I was still feeling unsettled about it. Ironically, although I was receiving good feedback, I still felt that there was something wrong. I talked to my sister Julie about it and she gave voice to the feeling I had but hadn't been able to put into words. So, less than three months before my publishing target date, I went back into it and *completely reworked* the manuscript. I was finally relying on *my own* opinion because I *am* the Decider!

7

Adventures on the Path

"Being born in a duck yard does not matter,
if only you are hatched from a swan's egg."
~ The Ugly Duckling ~
Hans Christian Anderson

The Fool

Too often I found myself returning to the same childhood scene and wondering, *haven't I already dealt with this?* I have learned that I could derive many conclusions from a single incident in my childhood and that each conclusion produced a feeling that would eventually lead me back to the incident, perhaps many times, until the healing was complete.

The manuscript for this book seemed ready for my editors. Yet it seemed something still wasn't right about it. I felt it might be "okay" or "good," but I wanted it to be *great*. I was riddled with doubts. I'm not a psychologist! What was I doing trying to write a book like this? What if I got it wrong?

I tried to contact my brother, a psychiatrist, who had already read the manuscript. I didn't reach him but if I had I would have asked, "I'm not making a fool of myself, am I?" It was a horrible feeling, but it was mine alone. I spoke with Natasha, now working on her PhD in psychology, who said, "Mom, you've been waiting a long time for someone to tell you that you have no business writing this book." She suggested I take my feeling down the Path.

I did. It didn't take long to name the feeling. It had come up several times already. I felt like a fool. I realized that, worse, I have felt this way, deep beneath my mask of composure and confidence, *for all of my life!* Much worse than feeling "incapable," I felt I was a fool.

Because of my fear of being seen as a fool, I had written the manuscript in a way that would ensure no one knew I was unqualified to write it. I had included quotation after quotation to support my ideas and give credibility to the work, credibility I feared I lacked. Ironically, in my efforts to prove the *opposite* of what I believed about myself, I was instead validating it. My inner child, who had concluded years ago that she was a fool, had somehow gotten into the driver's seat of the vehicle called My Life. I was horrified. This discovery made me feel so foolish! How could I have not known this?

I found a story from my childhood that could account for this feeling. I was not yet three years old, since my mother was pregnant with my brother, who was three years and three days younger than me. Mom had arrived home from the grocery store exhausted; so she lay down to have a nap, leaving most of the groceries right there on the floor. When she awoke, she saw my little sister and I sitting on the floor surrounded by slices of bread, each piece with the centers broken out – there were centers here, ends there.

She told this story with humour in later years. I don't know what she said when she discovered we had wasted a loaf of bread – was she angry, did she reprimand me, did she worry about the waste of money, was she frustrated because she would have to replace the loaf? I don't recall the look on her face. I do know that I was very sensitive and connected to her moods, which meant that no matter what she said, *I believed I knew how she felt.*

Did I feel like a fool? Probably. I had done something foolish, though I didn't realize it as I did the deed. I may not remember the incident well, but I do remember *that feeling*, because it was fear of having that feeling that had been driving me as I wrote this manuscript.

So I went asked myself what I wanted to feel. I wanted to feel Amazing, I wanted to feel Brilliant. "I am Amazing and Brilliant," I said. It felt wonderful!

Then two surprising things happened.

That day I received feedback from two of my readers – Alex, my son, and Stan Faryna, a fellow blogger. Both gave me valuable suggestions. Alex recommended that I include some guidelines for using the information. Stan said, "Don't hide behind the quotations. Tell the story from your heart."

They rescued my manuscript from the hands of a child and restored it into my hands. Their feedback sent the Fool scurrying away, never to return. When I asked Alex to tell me *point blank* what he thought of my work, he smiled and said he thought it was "brilliant." Stan, who could see the message beneath my numerous quotations, said it was "amazing." There were my Words! They had been there all along.

The Funeral

Usually when we hear a member of my large family has died, I don't think twice about it. I immediately make plans to travel to the funeral. But when I got the news this time, I was surprised to find myself resisting. Everyone assumed I would attend, but for some reason I didn't want to go. I didn't understand my reluctance, as it was completely out of character for me, so I walked with the feeling onto the Path.

What did I feel? I felt irritated, annoyed, and angry. The funeral was in a city three hours away and I was very busy. Maybe I wouldn't go. We have a huge family. Who would even notice if I wasn't there? But going was the right thing to do – I felt I *had* to go, and that bothered me even more. I know this sounds callous– *I was there!* I had to name the feeling to understand it.

Finally I was able to see it. I felt like a "good girl," *expected* by her family to do the right thing *all the time,* despite how I felt. It was as if the decision had been made for me before I even got the phone call. I had no choice. I was a "good girl," so my course of action was clear – except I didn't want to be known as a "good girl" anymore.

It wasn't hard to follow the feeling home. I was always considered a "good girl" as a child. Labels like this were common back then. It was meant to be an affirming label, but it felt constricting. It left no room for doubt; it left no room for my own will. It was a very strong label, heavy to bear – *and I was finished with it.*

What did I want to feel? The Word that felt right was "Good." I decided I wanted to feel Good. I am not a "good girl"; I am simply a Good person. I know it is very close in meaning, but to me it felt completely right. It was only after I had cleared the intolerable feeling that I was able to see things clearly and give myself permission to consider, for the first time, what I *wanted* to do. I wanted to go to the funeral.

My Own Little Bubble

No one has a perfect childhood. Even if I came from a "perfect" childhood, to blindly accept the personal worldview that I formed there is foolhardy because that worldview *was constructed by a child!* I was an "A" student, a "good girl," responsible. I had a happy childhood. Yet I still managed to distort and misinterpret many events that occurred when I was very young.

The problem was, I took everything that happened in my world very personally, as we all tend to do. But I have come to believe that nothing other people do has *anything* to do with me. My cousin put it in a funny way. He said, "Everyone is walking around in their own little bubble." I use this as a joke and people always laugh! It's the best kind of joke – the kind with truth in it. People laugh because they know it is true of themselves. I am the same – concerned with *my* affairs, deeply entrenched in my own life, and often oblivious to the effect my actions have on others, even, at times, the people closest to me. Why should I expect that my parents would have been any different? In exactly their situation, with their stresses and resources, I doubt that I would have acted differently.

It's not about blame. Blame doesn't help. It only wastes time. There is no value in pointing the finger. I prefer to fast-forward to the part where I take responsibility for how I interpreted what happened when I was a child. I hope my children will do the same when they follow their own feelings home to the childhood I co-created for them.

Whatever happened, happened. It's over now.

"Life, for instance"

Nothing was outside the realm of what I could heal by taking a walk down the Path. At one time I doubted this. I had a bad feeling about something happening in the blogosphere and thought this situation couldn't possibly apply. That's *business,* I thought. How could I take a business issue down the path? But at the essence of everything we do is how we feel. Every intolerable feeling has a message.

I started my blog, "Life, for instance," in November 2010 and for four months I wrote my heart out for friends and family and my posts received very few visitors and comments. In the fifth month, someone mentioned my blog on theirs and traffic began to pick up. Then someone else mentioned me in a comment on someone else's blog and more people came to my blog and commented. Suddenly I was getting so much attention I was blown away by it. Over the next two months my traffic continued to grow. There were more mentions and the rate of comments was increasing to impressive numbers.

Then one day I noticed no one seemed to be mentioning me on other blogs anymore. Worse than that, I found myself feeling *jealous* of those who were being mentioned by the bloggers who had raved about me and my blog just months earlier. This was a very uncomfortable feeling. It was becoming intolerable and it was *embarrassing!* After I had felt this way for a few days, I decided to try to take the feeling down the Path.

To understand what I was feeling I described how I felt in cryptic terms: *I had been receiving a lot of praise and attention, but then the spotlight stopped focusing on me and shifted onto others and I felt jealous of them.* When had I felt this way before? It became immediately clear. As a first-born child, I was celebrated and treasured but gradually, as three more siblings arrived, the attention I had enjoyed started leaving me and going to them instead. What I was feeling wasn't about what was happening in the blogosphere. It was about what had happened in my childhood!

Was I jealous then? You *bet* I was! Yet I had no *memory* of being jealous. This was an old feeling that had never been addressed. It still lived inside me and it was hijacking my emotions in a business situation that, amazingly, *perfectly re-enacted* the dynamic that had first produced my pain.

What did I want to feel? When I allowed myself to consider it, I realized I didn't really *want* to be the one who got all the attention. I wanted *everyone* to be happy. In the end the Word I found was "I am a Shining Star": I was not the *only* star in the sky, but holding my own in a sky filled with stars!

The Scene of the Pain

Even though I always felt different inside when I had worked through an issue, I was always surprised to see how the outer world reflected this change. The first time I noticed this was in Greece. The second time was at my parents' house when all of my siblings were home over the Christmas holidays.

In some way, any time I enter the family setting, I undergo a type of age-regression. All the childhood dynamics snap right back into place! It is as if the years peel away like pages from a calendar and again we are a bunch of kids at home with Mom and Dad.

It was only when I returned home from the gathering that I realized how different I had felt to be around my family. I hadn't expected to experience any shift in my relationships with my siblings. I hadn't consciously worked on sibling dynamics. Some of the issues I had cleared had turned out to be related to them, but my present-day relationships with them were fine. Yet being at home that Christmas, it was as if I was a different person in the midst of a different family.

I hadn't even told anyone what I had gone through. They didn't need to know in order to respond to me differently. They just did. They responded to who I had become, not who I used to be, because in so many ways I wasn't her anymore.

8

The Happy Place

"So please get your rags
And your polishing jars,
Somebody has to go polish the stars."
~ A Light in the Attic ~
Shel Silverstein

Remembering

I had not given a lot of thought, since I returned from
Greece, to the words Dawn had heard when she gave me
the treatment before I went on that momentous trip, although
they were the words that had started me on this journey:
"Where you walk, you will remember." All through those
nineteen days in Greece, I wondered what the message
meant; *what would I remember?* Choosing to forgo public
transit, Natasha and I walked everywhere in that beautiful,
fragrant spring climate. Just thinking about it now brings
back that peaceful feeling and makes me smile.

But the message was not about walking in Greece. It was about walking on the Path I discovered there. It was when I was on that Path for the first time that I remembered I am Mighty Excellent, the first of many wonderful discoveries made using the steps of the system.

Since then, I have walked the Path to confront my pain and name it. I have walked to Path to revisit my past and understand it. I have walked the Path into a present-day life of my choosing. Walking a Path to Peace has shown me the truth about my life and about me. It has helped me remember *who I am.*

Cape Breton

We were on vacation in Cape Breton the summer following our return from Greece. This was my summer place; it was the place I had visited nearly every summer since I was born, and where I brought my young family when Alex was a baby and Natasha was two. Being there had always been the high point of my year, the visit I looked forward to with longing and anticipation all of the rest of the year. It is my "Happy Place."

I was confused; I didn't feel as excited to be there as I usually do. I didn't feel happy and free. I couldn't understand what was happening to me. With all those Words written and tallied in my dog-eared notebook, I should have been feeling *better* this year – not *worse*!

We had been there for four days and I was no nearer to understanding this purgatory I felt trapped in. It was as if all my Words were crashing to the ground around me, like stars falling from the sky. And I didn't know why.

I finally decided to talk to Natasha about it. She peppered me with questions: how do you usually feel? What do you usually like about being here?

I usually felt excited to be there, where I am free to be who I am. I usually couldn't wait to get away from work and have a rest. But now, what I was escaping was my writing and my healing work – two things I loved. I had already had a rest in Greece, and with the claiming of each new Word I was more and more free to be who I am *at home*.

There it was! Coming to Cape Breton had always been the high point of my year, the place I longed to be for the eleven and a half months between visits. But with all the things that had happened to me since I began walking a Path to Peace, it no longer was the highest point – not because my Happy Place had depreciated in value, but because the rest of my life had risen to occupy the level of my Happy Place. Escaping no longer produced a feeling of relief because I no longer needed an escape. Nothing had changed but me, but that had changed everything.

I found my Happy Place where I least expected to find it – within me.

The End of the Story

I felt as if I was losing something very valuable *and I was.* Natasha, my precious daughter, was getting ready to leave again. She was moving to Ottawa to go to graduate school to continue her studies for the next six years. She would be home for visits during that time, but the thought of brief intermittent visits wasn't helping to soothe the grief I felt at losing her again.

The sadness I felt was so overwhelming that I couldn't think clearly. All I wanted to do was cry, so I let myself cry. I recognized the dynamic as one I had experienced every time Natasha returned home from university for a visit. I would begin to dread her departure on the day she arrived home. She would be here for a little while, but I knew I was going to lose her again. The pain of that knowledge was overwhelming.

As I watched her organizing her belongings and turning her attention to her new life in Ottawa, I felt as if she was slipping away. She was still in my sight, but she was preoccupied and unavailable to me. I was *right here* but I felt as if she couldn't *see* me. I felt impossibly invisible. I felt "lost."

I realized my feelings didn't seem to have words to express them because they came from a time in my childhood before I began to speak, a time when I didn't *have* words. I *remembered* that feeling – the feeling of a first-born child who was celebrated and treasured by her parents until the day when she suddenly no longer was the only child, when her little sister was born. Now, like then, I could only watch; I was feeling the pain of having had and lost such a wonderful one-on-one relationship with my mother and I was projecting this memory onto my relationship with my daughter.

What did I want to feel? It took some hard thinking, but when I found my Word, I knew. What I wanted to feel was "Found." I am Found as I see who I really am, a Mighty Excellent me despite all odds, and happy at last. I felt lost, but now, more and more, I am Found as I walk a Path to Peace, as I remember.

June 2011

Nearly a year has passed since the story ended. Today is a very special day. It is Natasha's birthday. Although she is meeting us in Cape Breton a month from now and although I have her presents bought and wrapped and ready to pack to take with us, I wanted to give her something special *today*.

Last night I had an idea. I could make a gift of my *Words*. My Words represent the best of what I want for her in life! Before I boarded that plane a year ago I had nine words. Now I have fifty-three. They are my birthday wish for you, Natasha, with love...

"You are Capable, Loving, Wise, Prosperous and Content. You are Healthy, Witty, Relaxed and Tactful. You are Attended, Free, Successful, Exuberant and Complete. You are Delighted. You're Living in Love, Living Your Dream, Truly Blessed and Beautiful. You are Celebrated and Treasured, a Winner; you're Okay. You are Found, Triumphant, Full of Integrity; Always You and [always] Loved. You're Deserving, Good, Supported, in the Know, the Decider. You are Here. You are Peaceful, Fearless, Empowered; Everything. You're Just as Valuable. You are Abundant, Okay on Your Own, Happy, Invincible and very much Provided for by Life. No Matter What You Do You Can't Fail. Things are Better and Better. You Make it Your Way. Everything in Your Life Flows. You are a Shining Star. You are at Peace. You Can Do Anything! You are Brilliant and Amazing. You, my precious daughter, are Mighty Excellent, too."

And as *Sittie*, would say, "Don't you *ever* forget!"

9

How to Walk the Path to Peace

"And will you succeed? Yes! You will, indeed!
(98 and ¾ percent
guaranteed.)"
~ Oh, the Places You'll Go! ~
Dr. Seuss

In this section you will find tools to apply the Path to Peace healing system in your own life. There is a review of the steps, a worksheet, word-integration exercises, lists of words, and stories. Although you can travel the Path on your own, you might also enjoy working with a partner or a group. For this reason I have included suggestions for walking the Path to Peace with a partner and guidelines for starting a book club.

Review of the Steps

Step 1: Naming the Feeling

Find the best word to capture the key feeling you are now experiencing. Keep searching for the name of the unwanted feeling until you have the "I feel" statement that describes the unwanted feeling you are addressing. Notice where you feel it in your body.

Question: What do I feel?

Step 2: Finding the Origin of the Feeling

Discover the origin of the unwanted feeling, or the reason you came to the interpretation/conclusion you did at a very young age. Follow that feeling to a place/incident/dynamic in your childhood that caused you to see yourself and your life in the way you do.

Question: When did I first feel this way?

Step 3: Choosing a Better Feeling

Look at the unwanted "I feel" statement and make a corresponding and empowering "I am" statement. Find the "I am" statement that empowers you and banishes the unwanted feeling.

Question: How do I want to feel?

Step 4: Integrating Your Words

Use the integration exercises for a minimum of twenty-one days to complete the integration of your new Word.

Review of Key Feelings

1. An unexplained "down," "off" or disturbed feeling upon awakening in the morning. This is a feeling that seems to be there before you have even had time to think.

2. A pattern. This is when you find yourself wondering why you always feel a certain way. It can be about a certain person – feeling jealous of someone, for instance. It can be a frustration, anger or sadness you feel much of the time. It can be a new pattern that you recognize occurring just two or more times. It can also be an all-pervasive, feeling-less feeling; it can seem like feeling nothing at all.

3. An overreaction. You see and hear yourself and you can feel that your response is over the top. It catches you by surprise and you don't know why you responded as you did.

4. A bad feeling resulting from something that happened that stays with you all day long or for many days. This could be a feeling of embarrassment because of something you said, or a feeling of regret for something you did.

5. An our-of-sync response. This differs slightly from an overreaction in that it can be a quiet response. You may find yourself feeling upset about something that you believe shouldn't bother you. You can't seem to let it go. You may be especially irritated at someone or something that happened. You feel it in your gut, and the feeling bothers you. You know when you have had an out-of-sync response because it just feels slightly "off" from what you expect you should feel.

Worksheet

Use this worksheet to keep you on track while moving down the Path.

Step 1:
How do you feel? Make an "I feel" statement about it.

How does [that word] feel?

What would [that word] say if it could speak? What would it scream? What would it whisper?

Continue asking questions like this until the "I feel" statement is achieved, accurately describing a feeling that evokes the deepest emotion.

Say it aloud. Where do you feel it in your body?

Step 2:

When did you first feel this way in your childhood?

What happened before that?

When did you feel that way before that?

Imagine if you could go back even further – what was your family like, your home, how many siblings did you have when you were born? What was the economy like? Where did your father work? Did your mother work? What was going on in the world (for instance, the Cold War, the economic crash, etc.)?

Step 3:

How do you want to feel?

What Word would describe that?

Is there a better Word that you could choose?

Say it aloud. Do you feel it in your body?

Step 4

Do the Pillow Work with the Flip Flop exercise for a minimum of 21 days.

"It can't be emphasized enough the importance of going beyond the feel-good statement to the actual practice, i.e., morning and night recollection of positive statements. Also critically important is the active negative thought interruption and more positive statement insertion. Otherwise this is only a feel good activity while being first uncovered and then you hall right back into habitual thinking. Knowing is not the same as doing. The world rewards action."

~Jennifer Lesperance

Key Feelings

- Invisible
- Stupid
- Incapable
- Ridiculous
- Foolish
- Needy
- Alone
- Overlooked
- Overwhelmed
- Responsible for everyone
- Sad
- Envious
- Overburdened
- Worried
- Ignored
- Disappointed
- Afraid
- I'm nothing
- Ugly
- Cast aside
- A loser
- Not smart enough
- Lost
- Abandoned
- Betrayed
- Dismissed
- Used
- Disempowered
- Not good enough
- Goofy
- Unattractive
- Awkward
- Loser

- Unsupported
- Unimportant
- Desperate
- Jealous
- Nervous
- Worthless
- Bitter

- Unlovable
- Scared
- Inferior
- Empty
- Colourless
- Insignificant

Empowering Words

- Brilliant
- Complete
- Empowered
- The Decider
- Free
- Amazing
- Here
- Everything
- Capable
- Love
- Incredibly Resourceful
- A Creative Genius
- Poised
- Classy and Cute
- Witty
- Relaxed and Calm
- Supported by the Universe
- First in my Life
- Exuberant

- Fearless
- Beautiful
- Celebrated
- A Winner
- Found
- An Astounding Success
- Loved
- Deserving
- Believe in Me
- Very Valuable
- Abundant
- Passionate
- Me
- Precious
- Resourceful
- Sexy
- Deserving
- Wonderfully Qualified
- Honourable

- Powerful
- Secure
- Okay on my Own
- Amazing
- Blissful
- Peaceful
- Adorable
- Magnificent
- Irresistible
- Glamorous
- Strong

- Mighty Talented
- Knowledgeable
- Self-Assured
- Bold
- Lucky
- Sensual
- Radiant
- Easy-Going
- Serene
- Mighty Excellent

Exercises for Integrating Your Words

In addition to doing the Pillow Work, you might find these exercises helpful in the integration process. The goal is to experience the *feelings* of your new Words so they become wired in your brain in place of the old wiring that you are allowing to atrophy.

The Visit Meditation

Picture the childhood home where you lived when you were about five years old. Recall the room where you played, the furniture, the colors, the smells. Imagine that you pay a visit to your younger self in that room. See your younger self playing on the floor and sit on the floor next to her. Introduce yourself and say that you are there to tell her that everything is going to be okay. Imagine her response. Tell her that she is smart, loving, strong, etc., going through your Words, one by one. Watch the child's face as you deliver this information. Feel the child's feelings, as she knows intuitively these things are true. Reiterate that everything is going to be okay, that she is valuable and special, and safe. Have fun with this meditation, letting your imagination guide you until it feels finished.

The Talk Show

Imagine that you have been invited to be a guest on your favourite talk show. You are standing off-stage and waiting for your cue. Listen to your host introducing you. Imagine that the introduction mentions each of your Words and elaborates on them in glowing terms. Walk onto the stage, take a seat to thundering applause and tell your story.

Do Lines

Remember in school when the teacher used to make us do lines? That wasn't fun; this is. Find some nice paper and a pen that feels good in your hand. Sit comfortably at a desk or a table and write out your Words in beautiful letters, making them statements that begin with "I am." If you know how to do calligraphy, use it, or make up your own lettering style. The act of shaping and seeing the Words will help you to integrate them.

The Yearbook

Bring to mind your graduation photo from your high school yearbook. Now imagine that this photo is at the top of a page in the yearbook. Give it a title, something like: "Our Biggest Success Story." See beneath it the article about you, complete with a glowing recitation of your Words and accomplishments. Enjoy how this feels.

Twins

In this exercise, think of your Words one at a time and bring to mind someone who personifies each one. It could be a friend, a co-worker, a sibling, a movie star or another famous person. For each Word, see yourself as being just like the person you admire, with the thought, "I'm like that too! It's like we're twins!" Stay with each quality for a moment, enjoying the way you feel with each one.

The Vision Board

Get a large piece of corkboard and decorate it with your Words. Place the board in a place where that you can go and soak up the energy of the feelings you are choosing, such as a meditation space, your bedroom, or by your computer. Enjoy the creation process, including cutting letters out of magazines or creating your own letters freehand or with stencils. Decorate the board with hearts and flowers, using colours that feel good to you. As you adopt new Words, add them to it. Creating this vision board will help you to review your statements on an emotional level whenever you see it.

Stories

These are stories of people dealing with different intolerable feelings and their journeys down the Path. The names have been changed and the stories used with their permission.

A Habitual Bad Feeling

Steffen was angry. He wanted to experience the Path to Peace, so I agreed to accompany and guide him.

Step 1: I encouraged Steffen to look beyond the anger to see what was hiding beneath it. He found more anger and a lot of determination. In him was a strong desire to fight to stop something that he could not name. He said the world was "wrong." He said he felt determined, exasperated, sad, and exhausted. At the bottom of all the feelings he had piled on top, the deepest feeling was *disappointment.* I asked him where he felt that in his body. He put his hand over his heart.

Step 2: Steffen knew where this feeling originated. He told me a horrible and sad story of something that had happened to him when he was very young. He received a punishment from his father that was completely out of sync with a crime of which he was completely innocent. His father had disappointed him. It wasn't the first time this had happened, but it was the time that stood out in his memory.

Step 3: I explained how his brain would have been wired in response to such a frightening experience and how so many conclusions would have been born of that event. Steffen saw how this had sparked his desire to stop injustice in the world, to focus his will and try to help, and to bring the world back into harmony. The pain of a little boy's world had been projected onto the whole world and this was the reality out of which he lived his life. I asked him what he *wanted* to feel. He said, "I want to feel joy."

A Pattern

Sherry's husband seemed so excited whenever his brother called. This bothered her, and she didn't know exactly why it did. He seemed so light and happy when he knew he was going to see his brother. Why didn't he seem this way about other things, especially things that had to do with her? This unwanted feeling seemed to rise in her whenever the brother called; it was a pattern.

Step 1: How did Sherry feel? She felt replaced, de-throned, passed over. The statement that captured the emotion for her was "I feel passed over."

Step 2: When in Sherry's childhood had she felt what she was feeling right now? Put in cryptic terms, the question was this: when did a brother take an important man's attention away from her, leaving her feeling "passed over"? Of course, the important man, as represented by her husband, was her father, and the brother represented the first-born male in the family, which removed her from the single-child throne to make room for the first-born son.

Step 3: What did she want to feel? That was easy. Sherry wanted to be first, but, not literally – she wanted to *feel* first in *her* life. "I am First in my Life" were the Words that captured that feeling. It felt wonderful, affirming that she got it right. "I am First in my Life!" These are powerful words.

When you feel first in your own life, you don't have to be first in the life of anyone else.

A Bad Feeling that Does Not Go Away

Margie felt guilty whenever anyone gave her anything. If something was given to her and not to her siblings, she felt bad about it. She could not accept praise unless it was equally doled out. In fact, Margie had trouble accepting much of anything. It was as if she feared taking up too much space in life. Even her demeanour was muted and quiet.

Step 1: Guilt was the unwanted feeling; "I feel guilty" was the statement that described her feeling and would provide the key.

Step 2: When Margie looked into her childhood to see where this feeling originated, she saw it in the dynamic of her home when she was an infant. Remember that at this step, the important thing is to understand that *something* happened that might have been the cause of how you were feeling today. We knew she had been a colicky baby because her mother had told her. Her parents were young and lived with her mother's parents. In the family home were many people who had to get up early to go to work in the morning. We knew that her mother, a young parent, needed to quiet the colicky baby so that others could sleep. Here is a tiny new baby, absorbing her mother's anxiety, feeling somehow that she was an inconvenience; that she had to be small and quiet and not "take up" space. This was an intellectual leap for Margie, but it completely resonated with her. She could feel it in her stomach.

Step 3: Margie searched for the feeling she preferred to feel instead of that one. It wasn't easy, because even for this task, she was more comfortable accepting a small word. But big, grand Words help to initiate the rewiring because they get the brain's attention. She needed a dazzling, empowering Word, one that brought with it an emotional charge strong enough to replace that unwanted feeling she had been feeling her whole life. She finally came up with "I am Ecstatically Embraced." Margie could feel this wonderful feeling in her stomach where seconds before, the old feeling had resided.

An Out-of-sync Feeling

Francine's husband did not seem at all interested in what she was saying. She could feel it. She was talking, but he wasn't really listening. It wasn't anything new. They had different interests, she knew that. So why did it bother her so much *now* when she had been aware of it for some time?

Step 1: She named the intolerable feeling: "I feel unimportant."

Step 2: Where did this feeling come from? When would she have felt this way in her childhood? It wasn't difficult. She was the oldest of six children. Garnering the attention of Mom or Dad was not an easy task. Throughout her childhood and adolescence, Francine became a bit of a drama queen, returning from school with big stories to share that always began with, "You're never going to believe what happened to me today!" Children need a lot of attention from their parents; this attention was usually not forthcoming in the larger families of the past. This need to be seen and heard had been carried into her marriage. In the more than twenty years she had shared with her husband, Francine had never noticed it. She had finally noticed this tendency because she was ready to heal it.

Step 3: What did Francine want to feel instead of unimportant? She wanted to feel good without needing the attention of others. She wanted to feel good *no matter what was happening.* She wanted to feel complete, no matter what was going on in the lives that touched hers. "I am Complete" was her Word.

Note: I read somewhere recently that one of the worst lines to ever come out of a love story was this: "You complete me." This is so misleading. If it takes someone else to complete me, will I be only half a person when he is away? I want to be complete, no matter what, no matter who is with me – even when I am alone.

Working with a Partner

Having a support partner gives you the gift of a witness to help you stay on track. The support partner's role is that of a facilitator, someone before whom you hold yourself accountable. It isn't necessary to choose your best friend or spouse for this role, as it is more important that it be someone who will be comfortable being honest and forthright. Your support partner must be someone who is capable of pulling you out of the mud when you find yourself stuck in it, even when you don't notice that you are stuck.

There are many great ways to stay in touch with a support partner today. The following are a few of the options. Combine the ones that will best work for you and your partner.

1) Meeting face to face

2) Connecting by phone

3) Communicating through email

4) Meeting through video chats like Skype, iChat, Google+ hangouts, FaceTime or Windows Messenger

You may decide to meet weekly and check in with email at regular intervals or meet bi-weekly with a video visit during the off week. Your plan may include brief daily emails affirming where you are in the process, i.e., did you integrate your latest Words, are you working through an unwanted feeling today, are you experiencing the effects of the changes within you in your world? Whatever format you decide to use, commit it to your calendar and honour it. We tend to drop the most personal practices when we become busy, taking a backseat in our own lives. Don't let this happen.

Keep a record of your progress on the Path. Use the worksheet to work through the intolerable feelings as they arise and prepare to share your successes with your support partner during your next contact.

Starting a Book Club

There have been few experiences in my life as enriching as being part of a book club. There is magic in a group like this, as it can provide support, community-building, and a sense that as we travel down life's sometimes bumpy roads we are not alone. If you have never participated in a book club, you're in for a treat!

It is always easier to see someone else's story clearly. When it comes to our own, we have selective blindness. We have become so accustomed to the lenses through which we view life that it is hard for us to see it in any other way. It can be extremely beneficial to walk the Path with a book club because of the different perspectives and personalities within a group. Additionally, forming a club around a common intention often leads to the forming of a true community which becomes a safe place for healing.

By the time my first book club for *The Road Less Travelled* met for the first time, I had already read another book by Dr. Peck entitled *The Different Drum*, which is a wonderful book about community building. As my group evolved through the stages of community building, I was able to recognize and identify each stage as we achieved it. The second time I formed a book club, this time focusing on *The Dark Side of the Light Chasers* by Debbie Ford, I watched as this group, too, became a community.

It is beyond the scope of this work to outline what Dr. Peck has so eloquently described in *The Different Drum*, but his definition of community is worth quoting at length:

If we are going to use the word meaningfully we must restrict it to a group of individuals who have learned how to communicate honestly with each other, whose relationships go deeper than their masks of composure, and who have developed some significant commitment to "rejoice together, mourn together," and to "delight in each other, make others' conditions their own."[1]

Building a community takes time. It is a delicate and beautiful process; one can be the bi-product of a group of people with a common cause gathering regularly to discuss their progress. When a book club moves into the community stage, it becomes a safe and healing place.

The Plan

Choose several people you would like to gather with and let them know you are forming a book club. Ask them to read the book to see if it "speaks" to them. If you can, make sure the group is made up of an even number of participants. This will be helpful if you want to arrange for everyone to have a support partner within the group.

Consider that since you will gather in your home and the homes of other members, you should make sure the group is neither too large for your seating area, nor too small to divide into two or three smaller groups. Set a date for your first meeting. Ask everyone to bring their copy of the book, a pen and a notebook.

The First Meeting

It will be important to allow some time for everyone to get acquainted at the first meeting so that they begin to feel comfortable with the group. Ask everyone to introduce him- or herself and to share the reason for deciding to join. It may take a pioneer or otherwise brave soul to begin the discussion. When I start a book club, I assume that person will be me. If you decide to have support partners, establish the partnerships at the first meeting.

The Support Partner

In addition to meeting at regular intervals, you may want to institute a method of staying on track *between* meetings. If you have an even number of members, you can pair off. If you have an uneven number of participants, one group will have to have three people who each will be support partners to the other two.

The Format

You may want to set some time aside at the beginning of each meeting to discuss a section of the book and discuss them in order to come to the fullest understanding of the theory and how the steps on the Path work. You may then want to take turns sharing your experiences on the Path.

The Witnesses

One of the most beautiful aspects of walking a Path to Peace with a group is the role of witness. So often when we share a problem with a friend or partner or parent, all we really want is to be heard and validated. Knowing there is someone in your life who really sees you can help make even the most intolerable situations bearable. A group of caring people who have gathered to make this journey together can be a perfect set of witnesses to our pain, collaborators in our efforts to heal, and a cheering section when we get to the end of the Path. We are inspired by the courage of the members as we watch them work through their issues. Most of all, we are relieved to know that others are with us on this journey – that we are not alone.

The Caution

In the beginning, there will be a tendency to want to "help" others in the group. I don't see this as the role of the members at all, as it may perpetuate in certain members the feeling of powerlessness with which many of us emerged from childhood. Scott Peck describes a true community as a group consisting entirely of leaders, because no one person seeks to help, heal the others. The roles of the members are to listen and affirm. It is the loving, listening presence of the members that gives us the courage to persevere.

However, the gentle questioning of others, if handled respectfully, may be beneficial. We keep one another on track without taking over and driving the car.

In this scenario, suppose one person, Rebecca, begins like this: "I woke up feeling depressed, so I went through Step 1 and discovered "I feel bored." That makes sense, because I have been off work on sick leave and unable to do very much. So I chose the Word "Productive" and got my husband to get a pile of books for me at the library on kitchen renovations, and now I'm making plans."

Nancy, noticing that Rebecca skipped Step 2, says, "You found that your unwanted feeling was 'bored.' What does 'bored' feel like?"

Rebecca replies, "Well, it feels empty, I guess."

Mary pipes in with, "How does 'empty' feel?"

Rebecca, now visibly uncomfortable, thinks about it and admits, "It feels useless. I feel useless. I'm not doing anything useful, just lying around trying to let my body heal."

Nancy asks, "How does 'useless' feel?"

Rebecca pauses, looks down and says, "I feel valueless. I feel that there is not any value in me as a person – only in what I do. And while I'm home sick, I'm not doing anything!"

The members can see by the look on Rebecca's face that she has hit upon something not merely intellectual, but also emotional. They wait in solidarity while she thinks about it. "Bored" did not elicit the "Aha!" feeling to indicate that she had captured the unwanted feeling. "Valueless" does. Someone asks her where she feels it in her body.

Someone else nudges Rebecca to Step 2 by inquiring when she felt valueless during her childhood. And thus the group accompanies her through the steps.

The group interaction keeps us authentic. If we are honest, yet kind, we can encourage one another get to the heart of the issues. If there is pain, we share it; if there are tears, we pass the tissue and sometimes cry together. In a group such as this, we do not feel alone.

The Talking Stick

In some book clubs, a "talking stick" is used as a visible reminder for the group to forgo interruptions and allow the speaker to complete his or her turn. When someone has the stick, others are permitted to interact with her, but only about her situation and with her permission, and never changing the subject.

Note: You might create the talking stick together by asking each member to contribute ribbons, feathers, etc., and decorating a stick that you provide. This would be a good activity to do at the first meeting.

Book Club Guidelines

Establishing clear guidelines is a great way to keep a group on topic. The following suggestions, if adopted by your group, should be reviewed periodically at the beginning of the meetings.

1) Our function is to be a listener, not a helper. Listening and validating is the greatest "help" we can give to one another.

2) This is a group without a leader; it is a group of all leaders. Everyone's unique gifts should come to the table.

3) When someone holds the talking stick, they have the floor. The person holding the talking stick should respect the time and stay on topic. We strive to share the rime we have as equitably as possible.

4) We agree that what happens at meetings stays at meetings. This means we don't discuss anything that happens here outside the meeting – not with our life partners, and *not even with another member of the club.*

5) We don't judge but accept and celebrate the courage of the one who shares his or her story.

Gratitude

I would like to thank my readers for sticking with me and for providing feedback at all stages of the writing (and re-writing) of *The Happy Place*: my friends Lisa Stoddard, Sarah Lord, Stacey Hughes, Jillian Ross Hebb, and Laura Ross and my nieces Melanie Thompson, Jessica LeBlanc and Erica LeBlanc.

I owe a lot to my editors, Jennifer Lesperance, Cindy Parlee, Alicia Versteegh and Amy Fox. And to Constantin Bechetaru for all his help with the cover.

I'm grateful to my siblings: Julie LeBlanc, who gave me some of the most valuable feedback, Dr. Allan Abbass, who contributed his professional opinion, and Stacey Johnstone, who has believed in this writer since she was four years old.

I would like to thank my husband for his support through the many Saturdays when I sat at the kitchen table more engaged with my laptop than anything else. I am indebted to my dad, Tony Abbass, my fastest reader and my biggest fan.

Finally, I want to thank my daughter and son: Natasha, who convinced me from the start, with a few words, that this project should go forward, and Alex, who, months later, with strangely similar words, encouraged me to see it through to the end.

References

1. M. Scott Peck, *The Different Drum: Community Making and Peace* (New York: Touchstone, 1987).

Other Wonderful Works

Note: Several times in this work I refer to Anthony de Mello. Though I never knew him but for his video tape program, I consider him to be my most beloved spiritual mentor. This is the video program to which I refer: Anthony de Mello, *Wake Up! Spirituality for Today* (Tabor Publishing: San Diego, 1967).

M. Scott Peck, *The Road Less Traveled: A New Psychology of Love, Traditional Values and Spiritual Growth* (New York: Simon and Schuster, 1978).

Joe Dispenza, *Evolve Your Brain: The Science of Changing Your Mind* (Deerfield Beach: Health Communications, Inc., 2007).

Richard Carlson, *You Can Be Happy No Matter What: Five Principles Your Therapist Never Told You* (Novato: New World Library, 1992).

Louise L. Hay, *You Can Heal Your Life* (Carlsbad: Hay House, Inc., 1999).

William V. Pietsch, *Human Be-ing: How to Have a Creative Relationship Instead of a Power Struggle* (West Port: Lawrence Hill & Company Publishers, Inc., 1974).

Debbie Ford, *The Dark Side of the Light Chasers: Reclaiming Your Power, Creativity, Brilliance, and Dreams* (New York: The Berkley Publishing Group, 1998).

Don Miguel Ruiz, *The Four Agreements: A Practical Guide to Personal Freedom* (San Rafael: Amber-Allen Publishing, Inc., 1997).

Neale Donald Walsh, *Conversations With God: An Uncommon Dialogue [Book 1]* (New York: Putnam Adult 1996).

Joseph Murphy, *The Power of Your Subconscious Mind* (Englewood Cliffs: Prentice-Hall, 1963).

LORI GOSSELIN

About the Author

Lori Gosselin has a Bachelor of Arts degree from Dalhousie University in Halifax, Nova Scotia, Canada. After graduating, she operated a number of different businesses ranging from calligraphy to Internet marketing, with Reiki energy healing work in the middle.

Finally she returned home to the place where her passion lived. By then there were two passions beating within her heart – helping people to be happy and writing.

The Happy Place was not the kind of book she dreamed of writing all those years when she was too busy raising a family and running a business to write anything longer than a short story. But the muse comes in mysterious ways. And when she calls, a writer answers.

She lives with her husband in the country outside of Moncton, New Brunswick, Canada. Connect with her at her blog: lifeforinstance.com. She hopes this book will help you to find the Happy Place in your life.

www.ingramcontent.com/pod-product-compliance
Lightning Source LLC
Chambersburg PA
CBHW071055040426
42443CB00013B/3341